D0793137

River Salmon Fishing

Bill Stinson
Illustrations by Pete Rehnberg

Frank Amato Publications, Inc.
P.O. Box 82112
Portland, OR 97282
(503) 653-8108

Contents

Dedication

This book is dedicated to fishing wives in general and mine in particular. Not ony does she help me get ready for my adventures, and patiently listen to my fish stories when I return, but she types up my manuscripts when I decide to record my experiences on paper. A treasure like this is very rare.

Cover illustrations and fish drawings on pages 14, 21, 22, 25, 27 and 29 by Ron Pittard. Used with permission of Ed Lusch. Color charts of these fish available from Windsor Publications, 2515 Windsor Circle, Eugene, Oregon 97405. Illustrations on pages 4, 15, 16 and 23 from the pamphlet *Anadromous Fishes of California*.

© 1986 Bill Stinson
ISBN 0-936608-46-3

Printed in Hong Kong
Book Design: Joyce Herbst

Cover photo: Larry Palmer, past president of the Association of Northwest Steelheaders, with a nice Clackamas River spring Chinook. Photo by Nick Amato

Introduction

The various species of Pacific salmon that migrate into the numerous rivers of North America were originally identified by the inquiring German, Georg Steller. His first scientific efforts were conducted on the wild rivers of Siberia when he was in the employ of the Russian government.

In 1741, while still serving Russia, he accompanied adventurous Vitus Bering on an expedition to the Alaskan Peninsula. Here, he re-identified the same five species that had been encountered on the Russian streams several years before.

Another German, Johann Walbaum, latinized Steller's names for the different species in 1792.

In 1861, an American ichthyologist, George Suckley, assigned the genus *Oncoryhnchus* to the group in order to distinguish them from *Salar*, the Atlantic salmon.

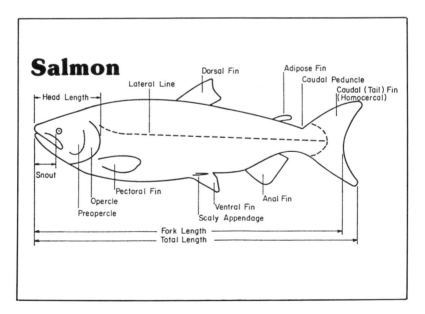

Salmon

Lateral Line · Dorsal Fin · Adipose Fin · Caudal Peduncle · Caudal (Tail) Fin (Homocercal)

Head Length

Snout

Opercle · Pectoral Fin · Preopercle · Ventral Fin · Scaly Appendage · Anal Fin

Fork Length
Total Length

The Sea Journey

Descending young salmon entering salt water after leaving their natal rivers sort themselves out according to species. Tiny pink and chum fry are forced to remain in the relatively protective estuary environment until they have sufficient size to battle the currents and hazards of the open ocean. Their small mouths permit feeding only on tiny plankton and the smallest of crustaceans. As they increase in size and develop strong jaws and teeth, they move out into the abundance of the open sea and add a variety of fish life to their diet.

Sockeye salmon are larger when they enter the salt because they have spent one to three years feeding in fresh water. They immediately move toward the northern and western Pacific and begin feeding on the multitudes of plankton and krill species.

Chinook salmon smolts have usually spent several months in fresh water and are well suited to transfer to a saline environment. Initially, they feed on small organisms but as they grow larger will devour sea life of substantial proportions.

Coho salmon smolts enter the ocean as the largest and most developed of the young salmon. Most wild races have spent a year aggressively feeding in fresh water. In a few cold Alaskan rivers, the fresh-water stay is prolonged to two years in order that they may attain the size required by their species to cope with the hostile elements encountered in the salt. The time required to reach smolthood is determined by size rather than age.

Many predators await the vulnerable young salmon. Seals, sea lions, otters, sea birds, killer whales, and larger fish are all eager to dine on the silvery juveniles. As they gain size, the fish will be confronted with the nets and troll gear created by man.

Depending on the species, the circling of the Pacific can continue for years and may cover thousands of miles. Salmon are in constant motion, swimming, feeding, and avoiding predators.

The size achieved by a member of a race within a species will be determined by the availability of food and the speed of maturation present in the genes of the individual fish. The fish continue to grow until they move into the beckoning flow of their home river.

To the unpracticed eye the five species of salt-water dwelling salmon appear much the same. Their backs are dark, almost black, blending to dark blue or green. Their sides are the brightest chrome. Bellies gleam a silvery white. Chinook, cohos and pinks have black spots on their backs. These physical characteristics change dramatically as salmon re-enter fresh water to spawn.

Fresh Water Hazards

Before the coming of man, migrating salmon were impeded by rapids and waterfalls. These natural obstructions tended to separate the species and provided a weeding out process that

Five Salmon Species

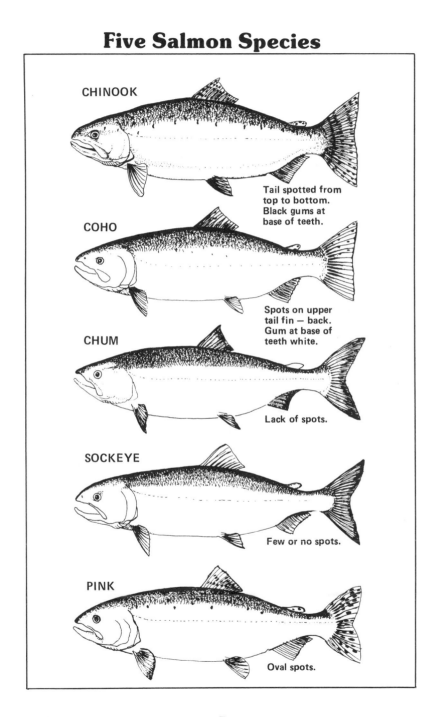

CHINOOK

Tail spotted from top to bottom. Black gums at base of teeth.

COHO

Spots on upper tail fin — back. Gum at base of teeth white.

CHUM

Lack of spots.

SOCKEYE

Few or no spots.

PINK

Oval spots.

River Salmon Fishing

eliminated the weakest. Drought and flood were also among the influences that regulated salmon populations. Bears and otters ate a relatively small number.

The Indians preyed upon salmon with all of the intensity

Alaska Indian-caught salmon being dried.

that could be applied with their primitive equipment. Over the centuries their fishing became more efficient, providing subsistence to the growing populations of red men who lived within the range of the salmon migrations. Their primitive fishing techniques, limited trade efforts, and unsophisticated methods of preserving the meat helped prevent overfishing.

Early arriving white men were quick to realize the commercial value of the multitudes of salmon. They attempted to trade with the Indians for the fish. When they discovered that the Indians were able to produce little more than they consumed themselves, salmon traders set about harvesting the fish with their own labor and equipment. Nets were imported and fish traps and wheels were constructed and installed. The white man's greed, superior equipment, and lack of any conservation ethic quickly reduced salmon numbers.

The fish population continued its downward spiral as human exploiters killed every salmon they could catch. They canned or salted it, and shipped it to some distant corner of the world. As the market became glutted, prices declined and the fishermen thought it necessary to catch and ship more in order to maintain their level of income.

Overfishing was bad enough by itself but man soon decided to completely restructure the lands and watersheds that God had created. Extensive logging, dredging, mining, irrigation, agriculture, road building, pollution, and dam construction caused changes to the water quality and impediments to migration.

Still, some salmon survived. In populated areas runs of fish are maintained with the help of an increasingly efficient hatchery system. In remote districts where the spawning grounds are still undamaged, salmon can reproduce in the wild in sufficient numbers provided some restraints are placed on commercial and rod fishermen.

Maturation

A variable rate of maturation tends to cushion four of the five species from natural disasters. If the eggs or fry of a particular year's spawning efforts are destroyed, fish returning on a staggered timetable from other years' offspring will repopulate a river.

Only pink salmon are on a rigid two-year reproductive cycle.

River Salmon Fishing

Chinook have the widest range of maturation. Precocious males may be sexually mature in two years while the late bloomers may not spawn until their seventh year.

When salmon begin to ripen after their extensive wanderings at sea, some unexplained homing instinct will beckom them back to the mouths of their home rivers. Frequently, maturing fish will wait a few days while they re-acclimate to the freshwater environment. Some runs are forced to remain in the ocean or tidewater until a substantial rain raises their river's level sufficiently to allow their upstream movement.

The many watersheds available to salmon have subtle but unique characteristics that have resulted in the development of the various species and races within the species. Heavy, powerful rivers require the development of large, strong fish to negotiate their surging currents. Small, shallow streams might require a lighter fish to navigate their meager riffles.

Some species have been better able to cope with man's changes to the environment. A species or race may move into another's habitat if water conditions change. Because of its great range of maturation and adaptability to man's restructuring and destruction of the environment, chinook salmon seem best suited to survive in heavily populated areas. Coho, because of their more rigid life style, are having a more difficult time adjusting to man's environmental alterations.

Under natural conditions each stock develops a sense of timing which places the fish into their accustomed spawning area when water flow, temperature, and maturation are ideal for spawning, egg incubation, alevin emergence, and fry growth.

Before fish-blocking dams were built on the Columbia, salmon migrated as far as 1200 miles. Now their upstream movement is restricted to a few hundred miles. Current Columbia River spring chinook begin migration long before they are mature. They don't seem to be in a great hurry and take an average of 30 days to traverse the Bonneville Pool. The later running and faster moving fall chinook make it in about five days.

Today, on the undammed Yukon River, salmon still

swim as far as 2000 miles to spawn. Long running fish need large reserves of energy-producing fat to maintain their strength on these lengthy journeys. Salmon that spawn close to the sea are inclined to have a much lower fat content.

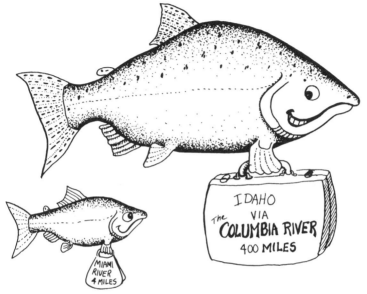

The five salmon species that migrate into our rivers have one overpowering instinct in common: they have come only to spawn . . . to play out their final role in Mother Nature's grand scheme. Soon after their procreation ritual is completed, salmon die. Their rotting carcasses create nutrients for the insect life on which the salmon fry and fingerlings will feed.

As ripening salmon enter fresh water their silvery sheen begins to tarnish and takes on the readily identifiable colors and characteristics of their species. With few exceptions, soon after entering their native rivers salmon lose their desire to feed. The speed at which they travel up their river depends upon the distance to the spawning grounds and their degree of ripeness.

When mature salmon arrive at their chosen spawning site, many fierce battles will be fought among pugnacious males to determine which will win the right to fertilize each nest prepared by the females.

The separate species seek different types and sizes of gravel in which to deposit and fertilize their eggs. Large, powerful chinook prefer coarse gravel. Their forceful tails are capable of moving stones several inches in diameter when preparing the redds. The smaller species choose finer gravel.

Water temperature is also a determining factor in the selection of the spawning area. Sockeye prefer cooler water than the other species.

When the pairings are complete and the ripe female has scoured out the nest, the two fish lie closely side by side. A forcible flex of the female's body as she presses herself against the bottom of the nest deposits several hundred eggs on the gravel. The waiting male simultaneously squirts a cloud of millions of sperm on the eggs. The sperm drifts away and dies in a matter of seconds, but if all goes well, most of the eggs will be penetrated by the tiny organisms.

When the spawning act has been completed, the ripe female moves upstream and with a few thrusts of her tail loosens enough gravel to cover the fertilized eggs lying on the bottom of the nest.

Subject to her whim and urgency, she soon prepares another nest in the same area. She may mate with the same male or with an eager newcomer.

Preparing nests and depositing eggs continues until her production is exhausted. Death soon follows.

Chinook Salmon —
Oncorhynchus Tshawytscha

C hinook are the largest of the salmon species and are the most vigorously pursued by anglers in fresh water. In local fisheries they are also known as blackmouths, kings, springs, springers, tules, and tyees. Chinook circle the northern Pacific for one to six years before making their spawning run into the rivers along the west coast of the United States, British Columbia, Alaska, Russia, Korea and Japan.

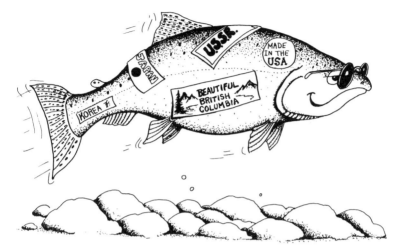

They have been successfully introduced into New Zealand rivers and the Great Lakes. Because their total population is only a few million fish, chinook rank number five in the salmon commercial catch.

Chinook may enter fresh water in any of the 12 months with spawning occurring from April into January. The mating ritual may take place within a few miles of salt water or, in th case of fish ascending the Yukon River system, 2000 miles from the sea.

Commercially, chinook weighing more than 120 pounds and measuring 5 feet in length have been taken. A species of this magnitude provides sport fishermen with some pretty significant incentives.

Chinook to over 90 pounds have been landed with rod and reel. The average chinook weighs 17 or 18 pounds; their size is gradually decreasing along the west coast of the United States because of the reduced size of hatchery-produced fish.

A three-year-old hatchery-produced chinook weighs 8 to 12 pounds. Twelve- to 18-pounders are usually four-year fish. Fish over 18 pounds are 5- and sometimes 6-year fish.

River Salmon Fishing

Wild fish that swim the unplanted and untamed rivers of Alaska and British Columbia attain an average size into the twenties. Precocious males join the spawning run when they weigh only a couple of pounds and are less than 20 inches in length. These jacks are Nature's insurance that at least some sexually mature males will be present on the redds to fertilize the eggs of spawning hens. If sufficient full-size bucks are available, they will usually muscle the jacks aside.

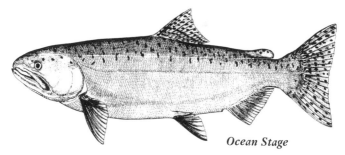

Ocean Stage

The nests of large female chinook are impressive excavations. The efficacious tail of a 40-pound hen is capable of extricating rocks five or six inches in diameter. She may in her nest building scour out a pit in the gravel approaching two feet in depth and several feet in diameter. She will deposit up to 5000 pea-size eggs.

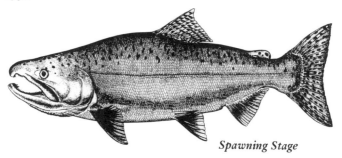

Spawning Stage

Chinook young may remain in fresh water for a few months or well over a year, depending on their race. The smaller smolts may linger in their estuary until they have sufficient size to tackle the rigors of the ocean.

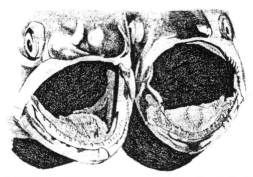

Silver salmon (left) have white gums around the teeth, while the inside of a king salmon's mouth is all dark.

Chinook are readily distinguished from the other salmon because of their blackish mouth and gums. Distinct black spots are sprinkled along the back and over the entire tail.

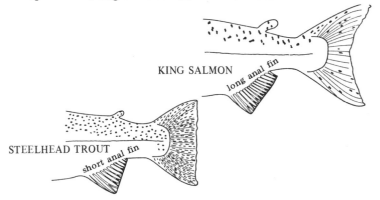

KING SALMON *long anal fin*

STEELHEAD TROUT *short anal fin*

ANAL FINS OF TROUT AND SALMON

On a salmon the base of the anal fin is longer, and there are more fin rays than on a trout.

Their color varies widely after they enter fresh water. In a single pool close to salt water, I have encountered chinook that ranged from bright nickel to copper to a pale rose. In some rivers, fresh fish have a gun-metal or purplish cast. Maturing chinook seem better able to maintain their brightness somewhat longer than the other species. The females will sometimes still be bright fish even though they have travelled hundreds of miles from the sea. As they near their spawning grounds, the females tend to turn rather blackish. Large males frequently develop dark red sides. Smaller males frequently darken to a brownish-yellow. The jaws and teeth of the males become very pronounced as they near the final days of their lives.

Chinook generally favor the deeper channels for their migration route. If heavy water is available they seem to avoid the shallower riffles. Fish caught in the tailouts are salmon that are pausing briefly after passing through some swift currents. The areas chosen for resting will usually be the deep, slower-moving pools of the river.

Fish that are contentedly ripening in deep pools near their spawning grounds are the least likely to open their jaws to crunch the fisherman's offering.

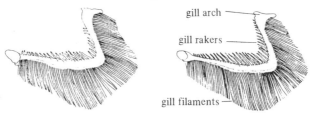

Salmon gill rakers. King salmon (left) have fewer and shorter gill rakers than the kokanee (right) or the very similar sockeye (not shown). The latter two are better adapted for straining small food organisms out of the water.

Water temperature and conditions determine when a race of ripening chinook enter a river on their spawning run. On river systems that don't freeze over, early running spring chinook may enter in January. These fish naturally use water that maintains a relatively low temperature and high content of dissolved oxygen during summer flows. Because their spawning time is months in the future, their bodies are loaded with fat to maintain them during the vicissitudes of the river journey. The very high oil content of these early runners makes them particularly attractive to the gourmet diner. Spring chinook offspring frequently reside in fresh water for up to a year.

Under natural conditions the runs rely on snow runoff and ice break-up to provide adequate water temperatures and flows.

Chinook can tolerate a maximum temperature of little more than 70 degrees. Water warmed to 80 degrees will be lethal to both adults and their offspring. Long-running fish will seek out the cool waters of their autochthonous tributaries where they will sexually mature over the summer months.

Rivers that maintain cool temperatures in their lower reaches during the summer have invited a summer race to develop over the centuries. These fish would tend to migrate somewhat shorter distances to accomplish their spawning mission. If adequate food is available, the young remain in fresh water for a considerable period.

This salmon was fooled by a plug.

In rivers that warm substantially during midyear, salmon wait for the cooler fall temperatures before entering. Fall chinook swim quickly to their spawning grounds and their bodies contain a relatively small percentage of oils. These fish usually complete spawning before the first of the year. Their young remain in fresh water for only a few months because they must avoid the lethal or uncomfortable high temperatures of summer.

River Salmon Fishing

In the southern part of their range many chinook wait until the winter months before migrating into their rivers. These late running fish spawn in the early spring and the fry find it necessary to descend almost immediately in order to avoid the summer's hostile warm temperatures.

Rambunctious silver clears the surface.

Chinook are powerful, enduring fighters. Their heavy bodies are capable of exerting considerable strain on rod, reel, and line. While not renowned as flashy, spectacular jumpers, an occasional fish will put on an impressive aerial show. Larger members of the species frequently take out several hundred yards of line and leave the frustrated fisherman staring in disbelief at the bare spool of his smoking reel.

Chinook, especially bright fish, readily take bobbers, crawfish tails, flies, herring, night crawlers, prawns, plugs, roe, sardines, shrimp, spinners, spoons, and combinations of the above. Many innovative anglers who want to appeal to all of the salmon's senses use a brightly-colored revolving bobber adorned with roe or shrimp or both.

* * *

Spring Chinook

My fishing companion, a frisky Labrador, and I were embarking on some steelhead fly fishing. It was Washington State's stream opener. We set out on the mile of river-edge trail leading to our favorite pool. About halfway along we passed a slow, clear bend that normally did not contain steelhead. For no apparent reason a large silvery fish started racing and cavorting through the shallows and finally went through the tailout and passed out of sight into the riffle below.

The fish was too large for this river's steelhead and I casually decided it must have been a spring chinook.

It turned out to be a fine, fishless morning. Many casts produced no strikes but the clean air and mountain scenery made it a great day to be alive.

Hunger pangs finally dictated the end of the fishing and we headed downstream toward the car for refreshments. As we noisily passed the bend where the fish had gone berserk, a crow hopped off the ground about 50 yards below and angrily gave us a good cawing. His behavior seemed a little odd and I was curious to see the object that our approach had forced him to abandon.

The ebullient Labrador bounded ahead and began barking excitedly. There is the middle of the path lay a beautiful 35-pound spring chinook. The immaculate fish was in perfect condition except that the crow had pecked out his eye. I sat down on a nearby rock for a breather and to think about the situation. Since the fresh fish hadn't been there when we passed earlier that beautiful morning, it was easy to surmise that this was the same fish that had spooked in the nearby bend. In his fatal panic he had shot through the shallow riffle and his momentum had carried his gleaming body far up on the stones of the gradual slope at the river's edge. His frantic flopping had removed him even farther from the water's haven. The stiff fish now rested a good 20 feet from the water. There the curious crow had found him and decided to dine on the most accessible portion of his hard, firm body: the eye.

Quickly searching my wallet, I failed to find my Salmon Punch Card. This was to be a steelhead trip and I hadn't bothered to check its whereabouts before departure.

Since this was the first day of the season, the game warden was likely to be around checking catches and licenses. The obnoxious crow angrily cawed from a nearby tree, demanding that we leave the fish to him, its original finder. The crow wanted it badly and was willing to wait until decay softened the firm flesh.

I ran an imaginary confrontation with the game warden through my mind. It was doubtful that he would believe the story and failure to possess a punched Salmon Card would probably result in my first fishing citation.

My frugal Scottish upbringing spurred me to a greater mental effort. My mind searched back to the last time that the card had been used. Sometimes I stored it in my tackle box and others it travelled in my wallet. Now I made a mental note to always keep it in my wallet in the future.

My last salmon had been taken from the Cowlitz River while fishing from the bank. Since I would have been utilizing a fishing vest rather than the boat-bound tackle box, the thing had to be in my wallet.

The new wallet had been a Christmas present and was an elaborate affair. There were many secret compartments where the owner could conceal keys, mad money, telephone cards, and numerous other small objects. A more exhaustive search finally revealed the misplaced card deep in the inner sanctum of the protective leather.

A quick punch and a scribbled entry and everything was legal. Fingers thrust through the gills, I lugged the prize fish to the car. The crow was furious, of course, but probably recovered within a few days.

Coho Salmon — *Oncorhynchus kisutch*

The scrappy coho are the second most popular salmon in our rivers. These marvelous fish are also called bluebacks, hooknoses, and silvers. Their dark, metallic blue-green backs are covered with black spots. The upper portion of the tail is also heavily spotted. The tail is squarer than the other salmons. The coho's white gums readily distinguish them from the black-gummed chinook. Both coho and chinook have black or dark tongues.

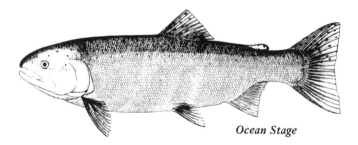

Ocean Stage

As they near maturity, the males develop a hook-like kype on their upper jaw. By the time the spawning ceremony begins, the males have become a deep, brick red. The females take on a dull bronze cast.

Because coho fingerlings usually stay a year in fresh water, their habitat is limited to streams that do not warm above 70 degrees. Most developing fingerlings mature into 6- or 7-inch smolts in about a year. Very cold water systems with limited

21

food may require a residence of two years before the little fish reach smolthood.

During the fry and fingerling portion of their cycle, young coho are very aggressive and territorial. They quickly drive off from their selected living areas intruding smaller salmon and trout.

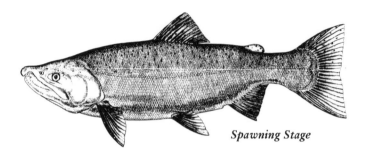

Spawning Stage

Coho inhabit much the same geographical area as chinook and have very successfully been introduced into the fresh-water habitat of the Great Lakes. Their wanderings in the salt are much less extensive than chinook. Coho typically spend two years at sea. A considerable number of precocious males and a few females return to fresh water as jacks and jills after only a year's feeding in the salt. A few fish will remain at sea for three years and account for some very large specimens.

The final few months of the coho's life are spent on a feeding binge. At this stage the salmon have developed powerful jaws and will recklessly attack almost any animal life small enough to enter their mouths. During their feeding frenzies they are particularly vulnerable to salt-water fishermen, both sport and commercial. In salt water coho rank number one in the sport fishery and fourth commercially.

Jacks and jills return as small fish of 1½ to 2 pounds. Two-salt-water fish range from 8 pounds into the high teens. Their size depends on the ocean's bounty and their genetic endowment. Coho have been landed on rod and reel in the 30-pound

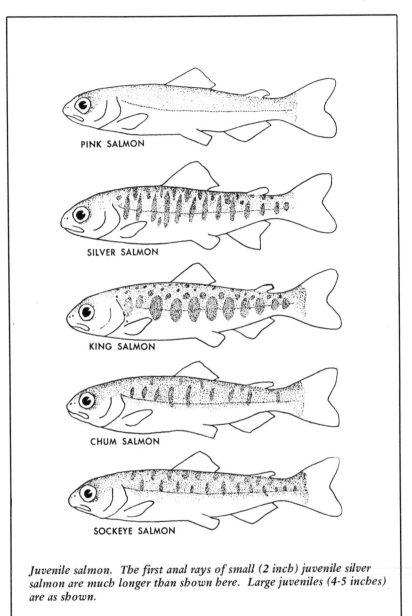

PINK SALMON

SILVER SALMON

KING SALMON

CHUM SALMON

SOCKEYE SALMON

Juvenile salmon. The first anal rays of small (2 inch) juvenile silver salmon are much longer than shown here. Large juveniles (4-5 inches) are as shown.

class. These heavy fish either lived three years in salt water or came upon a real bonanza on their feeding grounds. A large coho will approach three feet in length.

Spawning occurs anywhere from July to February and a large female will deposit about 3500 eggs. The spawning run may be a few miles or several hundred.

Coho retain some of their aggressiveness after they re-enter their natal rivers. They frequently take to the air and are the flashiest fighter of all the salmon. A fat bright fish has the capability of staging a spectacular show for the lucky angler.

Coho readily take bobbers, flies, plugs, roe, spinners, and spoons. They usually prefer to hold in the deeper pools and channels. If undisturbed they sometimes lie suspended 3 or 4 feet below the surface.

Chum Salmon —
Oncorhynchus keta

Chum salmon have been badly neglected by sports anglers. Not only do they eagerly strike flies, spoons, and spinners, but they are probably the strongest, pound-for-pound, of all the salmon. For many years a myth existed that these vigorous fish would not take lures in fresh water. Anyone who has fished where these combative middleweights are present would heartily disagree.

An increasingly popular chum fishery is building in the rivers running into Oregon's Tillamook Bay. Although a few remnants still move into the Sacramento River, the Kilchis and Miami rivers are about the southernmost portion of their range. Washington, British Columbia, Alaska, the Northwest Territory, the Yukon, Russia, Japan, and Korea all support runs of chum. They spawn in rivers further north than any other salmon.

Chum have widely varying spawning instincts and fat content. I have observed them trying to spawn in salt water on the beaches of British Columbia's Dean Channel. Others, laden with heavy deposits of body oil, migrate 2000 miles up the Yukon River. These long running fish are capable of swimming upstream against the river's heavy current for over 40 miles a day.

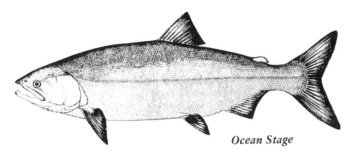

Ocean Stage

Various runs may enter their home rivers anytime from July until December after feeding in the salt for one to four years. Females prepare their redds from August to December and lay about 3000 eggs. The emerging fry descend toward salt water almost as soon as they leave the protective gravel.

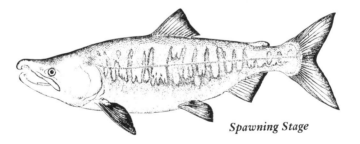

Spawning Stage

This species attains a size second only to the mighty chinook. Particularly large specimens may reach 40 pounds and be over three feet in length. However, the average will be closer to 10 or 12 pounds.

As they leave the sea, fresh-run chum are a very handsome fish. Some will have faint blackish blotches on their sides, while others will be completely silver. There are no black spots on the back or sides. Frequently, the anal fins will be tipped in white.

As the fish begin to ripen they develop pronounced reddish splotches on their sides. Their backs assume a greenish cast. Fearsome maws develop canine-like teeth as spawning nears.

In Alaska the Indians and Eskimos traditionally netted and dried the plentiful chum for their sled dogs. This bit of history along with the chum's mouthful of large teeth accounts for their nickname of "dog salmon." The more genteel and somewhat more descriptive term "calico salmon" is used in some areas.

Of all the salmon that I have encountered in fresh water, chum are probably the most aggressive toward artificial lures. In many rivers they hold in shallow water only a couple of feet deep. Chum action can be incredible on a sunken fly presented with a wet tip or floating line. At the peak of their run the number of fish hooked will be limited only by the physical endurance of the angler.

While not quite as flashy as coho, the chum runs are very strong and frequently punctuated with surface-clearing leaps.

Although not legal to pursue in fresh water in British Columbia, chum still rank third in the sports catch in their range. Their abundance in the salt also places them third in the ranks of commercially-caught salmon.

The flesh is a pale color but fresh from the sea is very delicious. Some clever fellows add a little red food coloring to their brine when they smoke these fish. This evidently makes them more psychologically acceptable.

Pink Salmon — *Oncorhynchus gorbuscha*

Pink salmon are the most numerous of all salmon and rank number one quantitatively in the commercial catch. They spawn in the rivers of Washington, British Columbia, Alaska, Russia, Japan, and Korea. They also have the smallest average size and usually weigh in from 3 to 5 pounds. A 10-pounder would be a whopper.

These fish are on a rigid two-year life cycle. There are no jacks and there are no three-year-olds. Some rivers have runs every other year, while others host a race of fish every year.

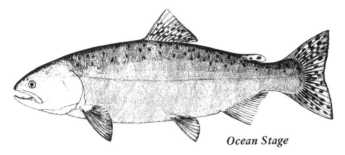

Ocean Stage

Northern British Columbia and Bristol Bay rivers produce pinks in even-numbered years. Other Alaskan streams and those in southern British Columbia and Washington maintain pink runs in odd years. The Skeena and Bella Coola river systems produce fish in both odd and even years.

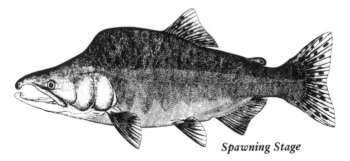

Spawning Stage

Pinks have large black spots on both their backs and tails. Their scales are very small and tend to rub off when the fish are handled. The males develop very large humps on their backs as they ripen in fresh water; hence their nickname of humpback or humpy. Mouths are light-colored.

Spawning runs occur from July to September; the redds are comparatively close to salt water. Females produce about 2000 eggs. The fry drift toward the sea as soon as they emerge from the gravel. This gravel of necessity will be rather fine because of the relatively small size of the adult fish.

Pinks actively pursue flies, spinners, and spoons. While not large enough to wage a prolonged battle, they do jump and give a good account of themselves on trout-strength tackle.

Sockeye Salmon —
Oncorhynchus nerka

Because they spend their lives feeding on tiny plankton, sockeye are the least inclined of the salmon species to open their jaws to engulf the angler's offering. Those that do strike probably do so out of anger or irritation. The objects that seem to produce most of the strikes are flies or wobbling plugs. Some rivers in Alaska produce a higher percentage of pugnacious biters than others.

A few favored Alaskan rivers support such huge numbers of these fish that if the angler keeps casting long enough he eventually encounters a biter.

Most of the sockeye taken in the artificial fishery created in Lake Washington are taken on deeply-trolled Kwikfish, Flatfish, or Hot Shots.

Numerically, sockeye are second in the commercial catch, but economically they are number one. Their beautifully textured red flesh is truly a gourmet's delight. Many millions of these fish are quick-frozen and shipped to Japan from Western Alaska. Most of the rest are canned and sold throughout the world as red salmon.

A few lucky sport fishermen get to enjoy the succulent flesh fresh from the home river.

Sockeye have no spots on their backs or tails. Their mouths do not have the large teeth of the other salmon species. The prominent eyes seem to be slightly out of proportion to their streamlined bodies. When ready to spawn the males develop a decided hump on their backs and their

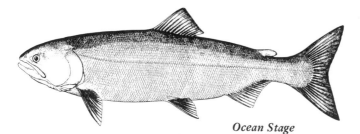

Ocean Stage

coloration changes from the silver of the sea to a bright red. The bright red sides are accompanied by a green head. The reddish coloration in fresh water and the deep red flesh account for their local name of red salmon.

The widely differing rate of maturation in both fresh and salt water provides for a variety of sizes of mature fish. Eggs from a single nest may grow into sockeye weighing 2 to 14 pounds. The average size is 6 or 7 pounds.

With few exceptions sockeye require watersheds that include a cold lake adjacent to their spawning area. The emerging fry move into the nearby lake soon after they leave their redds.

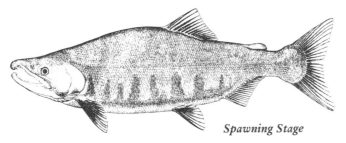

Spawning Stage

Sockeye young depart from fresh water on a staggered basis. Their journey to the salt will come at 1 to 3 years of age. A few never develop the urge to travel seaward and will spend their entire lives in a chosen fresh-water lake. A mature spawning sockeye may be anywhere from 3 to 8 years of age.

29

While growing in fresh water the fry and fingerlings provide food for resident trout and rainbows. Mature lake trout will even reverse the normal migration direction and follow the downstream moving fry toward salt water. In the spring, sea-run cutthroat trout will move into the lower reaches of the same streams for a feeding spree on the descending young sockeye.

In years that have large numbers of surviving adults, the spawning gravel can become glutted with sockeye eggs. Newly arriving females scour out nests in gravel already saturated with fertilized eggs. Displaced eggs litter the surface of the gravel. An average female produces about 4000 eggs.

The Columbia River is the southernmost river hosting runs of sockeye. The Columbia and Quinault runs of fish are known locally as bluebacks. In the Columbia system the numerous man-made reservoirs somewhat take the place of the usual cold lakes required by young sockeye.

* * *

Little Shuswap Lake was glassy smooth as I trod the boat dock on the evening of my first visit. A few hundred yards distant some angler-filled boats were beginning to gather where the imposing current of the Little River thrust itself into the waiting calm of the lake. During the previous fall the Little River had hosted thousands of spawning sockeye. The offspring had drifted into the lake to grow fat on the resident plankton.

The generous resort owner had provided me with two fly patterns. The smaller was a little over an inch long and represented sockeye fry soon after they gained their freedom from the protective spawning gravel. The other was a large streamer fully 3 inches in length and an excellent imitation of the sockeye smolts on their way to the sea.

There was no motor available for the tiny rented round-bottom boat but the anticipation of hooking one of the world-famous Kamloops rainbows pumped plenty of adrenalin into my rowing muscles.

The dinghy was soon speedily skimming across the lake's smooth surface and by the time I reached the river's influence the boat was really smoking. My momentum carried the little 8-footer well out into the current's flow and I was soon spinning through a bevy of anchored boats, largely out of control. The veterans in the other craft seemed slightly amused by the newcomer's embarrassed maneuvers.

Luckily, I navigated through the flotilla without a collision. As I restructured my composure, a large trout fractured the

surface as he slashed into a school of tiny sockeye. The fellow who had rented me the boat had casually remarked that a 15-pounder had been taken the day before. The larger fly was already knotted to an 8-pound leader. I cast in the general direction of the recent boil and slowly stripped in. Nothing happened. I slipped on my polaroids and peered into the water. Thousands, maybe millions, of tiny sockeye swam just under the surface. Two more feeders rolled off to my left. The fly landed about 3 feet from the nearest one. My shaking hands carefully stripped the line . . . again, nothing. The boat renter suggested trolling if the rainbows wouldn't hit the fly on the retrieve. I made my maximum cast off the stern. Several swirls broke the surface on the right. The rod was secured under my knee. I took three pulls on the oars and an incredible strike nearly tore away the rod. The reel shrilled and seized as it over-ran. The tip bent into the water and the leader parted. This violent action had lasted maybe two blinks of the eye.

I was learning the handicap of having only one reel along. It took an exasperating 30 minutes for my shaking fingers to un-ravel the tangled line. I drifted aimlessly far out into the lake, and the shouts from the anglers who were fighting fish from anchored boats became almost inaudible.

The fly line was at last smoothly respooled on the reel and the fry imitation knotted to the leader.

I pulled steadily toward the encouragement of the anchored boats. There was no action until the river's mouth was a hundred yards away and the influence of the current's power could be felt against the boat's frail bottom. Three bucking rods were visible in the anchored craft.

Attentiveness to my own rod had become a little sloppy because of the captivating excitement created by the lucky, nearby anglers.

A heavy jerk bent the fiberglass over the stern. The whirling reel handles thumped first my leg and then my knuckles as I struggled to gain control. We fought well into the purple gloom of the twilight before this rambunctious fat fish came to the side of the boat. In the dim light it was still possible to see the faint blush of rose that stained its lustrous side. As I tried to free the fry fly from his jaw without lifting him from the water, he regurgitated a dozen tiny sockeye.

The fly was deeply imbedded but with a gentle working back and forth it came loose. The fish was very docile for a couple of minutes while I held him slightly below the surface. Renewed, he suddenly flexed his sinewy body and departed into the protective depths. Darkness was almost gathered as I stroked for the distant dock.

Fishing Techniques

Spoons

A spoon worked slowly near the bottom has accounted for the demise of many a river salmon. All of the species will gobble the metal if it is presented at their level in an enticing fashion. Most fishermen cast and work spoons in the standard way: casting directly across the current and following the drifting spoon downstream with the rod tip. Somewhere in the lure's swing, the flashing metal is likely to sink to the fish's level and a strike may occur. I used this method myself for many years and hooked a fair number of fish.

On a visit to the Babine River I watched master guide and fisherman Ejnar Madsen cover a favorite lie with his big Kitimat wobbler. The cast was made directly across stream but as soon as the lure touched the water, the line was immediately fed to permit the rapid descent of the polished metal to the fish's level.

When the lure ticked the bottom, the rod was swung directly downstream. The reel handles were turned just fast enough to impart some action. Further along in the swing the current caused enough action and cranking was unnecessary. Each type of spoon imparts a different wiggle to the rod tip and a little experience is required to learn when they are properly working.

With this technique the highly visible full side of the wobbling metal is presented to the fish rather than just the stern end. Also, by immediately gaining contact with the bottom, the spoon is in the fish-holding portion of the flow a much higher percentage of the time. The heavier and deeper currents require casts upstream of the angler in order to reach the bottom.

Whether or not required by law, the replacement of the usual treble hook with a single siwash or Mustad 3407 or 34007 is urged. These should be positioned on a stainless steel split ring so that the point rides up.

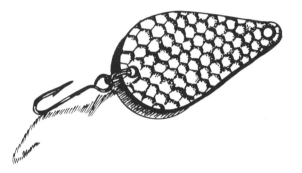

There is much less chance of the spoon snagging on the bottom and the single point seems to penetrate and hold the fish better than the treble. Singles cause much less trauma to the fish, if they are to be released, than the trebles.

Some spoons fish well on a snap swivel and some do not. If a spoon has a tendency to revolve, a high quality snap swivel may be necessary to prevent the line from becoming twisted. If the lure wobbles back and forth, a rounded Duo Lock or Interlock will best bring out its action. A small safety snap has a tendency to pinch the edge of the spoon and crimps its action.

The line can also be attached to a stainless steel split ring on the nose of the spoon. Knotting the line directly to the spoon is usually not a good idea because of the rapid abrasion of the monofilament caused by the spoon's movement.

River Salmon Fishing

A pair of inexpensive split ring pliers is a great aid in changing rings and hooks.

A word of caution is in order when the spoon is being reeled in after the drift has been completed. If no swivel is used the heavy force of the current against the rapidly moving spoon will probably twist the line. As soon as possible bring the spoon to the surface and skitter it over the top of the water while rapidly reeling in. When a rod's length of line is beyond the tip top, lift the spoon clear of the water and let it dangle for a few seconds. Most of the twisting occurs in the last few feet of line and the twist is removed with this maneuver. It is not a bad idea to remove the spoon once in awhile and allow a hundred feet of line to wash over a convenient riffle. By the time the line is back on the spool it will be completely straight and untwisted.

Anglers line up to intercept a run of reds at the mouth of Alaska's Russian River.

If conditions permit, a thorough coverage of the holding water can be accomplished by starting at the head of the pool and gradually lengthening the casts until the far side is reached.

As each cast is completed, the angler takes a step or two downstream. This method is particularly effective when the exact holding position of the fish is not known. Every fish in the pool will be given the opportunity to inspect the offering.

If this approach is not feasible because of the terrain or the presence of other anglers, a series of casts can be made from a single location. Many fishermen begin by exploring the mysterious water on the opposite bank, but the water is best covered by casting to the nearest fishing looking cover. The casts are gradually lengthened until all possible lies are fished. The system is repeated when a new position is assumed.

While salmon will lie in water that has some steady currenty, they frequently hold in completely slack water. Upstream, cross current, or downstream casts may be necessary and effective for fishing this quiet water. A little extra action can be imparted to the hardware with some movement of the rod tip.

* * *

Shortly after moving to Washington, I was invited to go salmon fishing on the Olympic Peninsula's Queets River by some avid fishermen. They had heard through the anglers' grapevine that the Indians had not been netting the river for some mysterious reason and the fishing was hot. We forded the river near the end of the road well up in the Olympic National Park as the July dawn was breaking. The oily surface of the tumbling unspoiled river with its clean gravel was about the fishiest looking water that I had ever seen. No railroad or highway marred its pristine valley.

My companions were all in excellent physical condition and set a fast pace up the trail through the beautiful old-growth timber. The towering firs and cedars shaded the sun and largely prevented the growth of any underbrush. It was possible to see a couple of hundred yards through the huge conifers. Twice we paused to observe herds of unfrightened elk.

River Salmon Fishing

My appendix had been removed only two weeks before and after a couple of miles I was clutching my incision. Since we had arrived in this unknown wilderness in total darkness, I didn't have the slightest idea of our whereabouts; keeping up with my companions was mandatory.

We walked the five miles to Spruce Bottom shelter in one hour flat. A quick conference was held and the decision was made that two of us should fish here. I quickly volunteered. The other three headed for a large salmon pool about three miles upstream.

Floyd was into a large king after only a few casts. Unfortunately his spoon was thrown during a short powerful run.

My throbbing side coupled with my fumbling fingers made rigging up difficult. The first excited cast was planted in an overhanging bush and the nickel-plated lure dangled helplessly. As I was breaking off, Floyd's stubby spin rod jerked downward as another large king seized his spoon. The frantic fish tore around the pool and after 20 minutes was eased up on the gravel. We had decided to release all fish caught on the first day because of our lack of refrigeration. The 20-pounder was gently pushed back into the welcoming pool.

The cavorting salmon had caused the other fish in the pool to go off the bite. We headed upstream in search of new water

As we trudged over a long, sloping gravel bar, we discovered the carcass of the largest salmon that either of us had ever seen. The immense fish must have weighed over 70 pounds fresh from the sea. There was considerable wishful discussion about how nice it would be to have such a giant on the end of a line.

The next pool was only half the size of the first and as we approached a large salmon rolled at its throat. My angry incision was really burning and Floyd easily out-distanced me to the waiting fish.

I decided to settle for the tailout. After I made a couple of casts, the wobbling spoon stopped halfway through the swing. A hard jerk set the siwash into a 6-pound jack chinook. This aggressive little fish bounced across the surface the width of the pool and then circled the bottom for five minutes before

The author with a five-year-old chinook. Bob Steele photo

coming in. Three more jacks up to about 8 pounds came to my spoon in this spot. All were released. During my prolonged activity, Floyd had taken a steelhead and a Dolly Varden. I walked along the bar on my way up to meet him and casually cast the spoon into the heavy water in midstream. The chunky spoon sank quickly and I was distracted by Floyd's carrying on about losing another fish. A salmon was waiting where the water deepened off the edge of the bar and the rod was almost torn from my grasp as the big chinook grabbed the spoon.

After a half hour's struggle, his movements became heavier, slower, and less certain, and the fish was beached and admired.

Since I had never caught a 25-pound chinook before, it was with some reluctance that I eased that beauty back into the water. Floyd assured me that we would catch plenty more like that one tomorrow.

I sat on a rock and admired the splendor of the place. White-capped mountains were veiled by the dense stand of big timber. An eagle soared in the distance.

Floyd kept casting but soon felt that we had exhausted the possibilities of this pool and wanted to head upstream. I decided that one more pool would be enough for my unhealed body.

By the time we came to the next drift I was about done in. Floyd started to cast and I reclined on a moss-covered rock.

Floyd hooked into a 30-pounder and asked if I would like to land it. I groaned and told him to go ahead. This bright, clean fish cleared the water three times before being beached.

As Floyd continued casting, I was convinced that any remaining fish would be too spooked to strike. Wrong again!

My companion's rod bent over and an incredible salmon wallowed and thrashed on the surface. The racket sounded like a couple of deer had fallen off a cliff into the river. The fish looked to be the size of the dead giant that we had seen earlier. Floyd boisterously shouted that he was going to land that fish or else. Thirty minutes later and a quarter of a mile downstream, he didn't sound as confident. During the fish's oceanward onslaught, Floyd had fallen on the stones a couple of times and his body was bruised and weary. He handed the bucking rod to me as we stumbled along, so that he could have a little rest. Twice during the next 15 minutes the spool was completely cleared when I couldn't quite keep up with the dogged fish as he lunged toward the sea. A short, painful sprint on my part would result in a few turns of line on the spool. Floyd took over again and we continued to alternately walk and trot after the seemingly tireless fish. Mercifully, we came to a large log jam that halted our downstream race. The spool was emptied, the rod pointed at the fish, and the line parted. Floyd and I groaned. Possibly for different reasons.

The oarsman tries to unravel three silvers hooked simultaneously.

We were at least a mile below where the fish had been hooked and since it was well into the afternoon, decided to fish our way toward camp. Actually, Floyd decided to fish while I stumbled slowly down the well-defined trail that paralleled the river. Shortly before dark I arrived at the ford and could see our car on the other side of the river. As the strong current rippled past, there was doubt in my mind that I would make it across. My four companions suddenly burst out of the trees excitedly discussing the many fish that they had hooked. I reluctantly swallowed my pride and explained my dilemma.

The three men who had gone upstream appeared to be as fresh as they were in the morning. One grabbed the rods and the other two steadied me across the gurgling flow. The battered Floyd was able to negotiate the quick current by himself. As they started to cook dinner I wearily crawled into my comforting sleeping bag and didn't regain consciousness until midmorning.

Spinners

Spinners may be fished much like spoons. Casting across the current and carefully working it with just enough tension to keep the blade revolving near the bottom will produce strikes.

Another very productive technique is to cast quartering upstream or even directly upstream, and allow the spinner to sink near the bottom. As soon as it reaches the desired level, the retrieve should begin. Knowledge of the spinner's feel on your rod tip is essential to ensure that the line is being cranked just fast enough to revolve the blade. If the tick of a rock is felt, an acceleration will be required in order to prevent snagging the lure.

There is a constant debate as to the best color or plating for spoons and spinners. Some anglers prefer copper or brass on dark days and nickel or silver on bright ones. Others believe just the opposite. The argument continues when the decision has to be made whether the finish should be plain, hammered, or scaled, or if a touch of bright paint should be added.

I'm not sure whether the salmon are concerned about the lure's color. Salmon have bitten my nickel offerings on dull and bright days and brass lures have brought strikes under widely varying light conditions.

* * *

A couple of years ago a friend sent a half-dozen entirely black french spinners. These were stuffed in my tackle box just prior to my departure for the famous Cedar Creek Hole on the North Lewis. As usual, when fall chinook are running the crowd is dense. We found a spot well upstream of the main body and tossed out the anchor.

There were no shouts of excitement from the hundreds of neighboring fishermen as we strung our rods. My eye caught a black spinner and I decided to knot it to the line. Hundreds of baits and lures cruised the beckoning waters.

The black beauty was barely visible as I dragged it through the murky water next to the boat. The clevis wasn't particularly free-running and considerable speed was required to make the blade spin. The first cast of the day sent it far out into the inviting current. It was allowed to sink near the imagined bottom. My speculation as to the water's depth wasn't accurate and the virgin lure promptly caught on an immovable solid object.

Since five more of these unproven spinners still reposed in my spacious box, the line was quickly snapped and a fresh one was tied on.

The retrieve was begun a little sooner and the whirling blade's action was felt on the graphite tip. The retrieve was uneventful for about 50 feet and then the spinner stopped. I struck hard and a 6-pound jack chinook came to the surface. Partner Bob had looked skeptical when he first saw the black spinner but now his face had the amused look of a man who had just witnessed a fishing fluke.

The fish was bright and went into the box. Thousands of casts by our neighbors plied the water in search of the fish believed to be lurking there. Crossed lines were tangled. Tempers flared. The competition was fierce. The tranquillity that we sought was not to be found here. No one hooked a fish. Bob suggested three more casts before we departed for a more relaxing and serene location.

The black spinner was cranked in twice more without incident. Just about convinced that the singleton fish was a fluke and not caring whether the metal was lost or not, I allowed it to sink until it ticked the bottom. The tip was raised and before the reel handle was turned three times, the rod was wrenched by a heavy strike.

The chinook was a real hell raiser and immediately swam for the center of the dense flotilla. Bob upped the anchor and we followed into the thicket of anchor ropes. Master-

fully, Bob steered around the unmoving boats. Several times
I felt my line grating on unyielding ropes or aluminum chines.

It was one of those unlucky fish that regardless of its
strength and tenacity finally succumbs to the waiting net. We
had drifted well below the famous hole in the landing process
and no more fish were encountered in the three miles to the
take-out.

Trolling

T rolling is a very productive salmon fishing technique in the
lower or slower-moving sections of rivers. In the larger
rivers where there is a tidal influence, it is about the only method
to use during slack water.

River Salmon Fishing

As a general rule, chinook lie or swim near the bottom of the river bed. The exceptions are a few large rivers where the fish will sometimes lie suspended 12 or 14 feet below the surface in very deep pools. Scientific type fishermen lucky enough to have a sensitive depth recorder will quickly become expert at the exact depth that the fish are holding.

Many of the old pros who fish the Willamette River rely on large, finely-tuned spinners to put the spring chinook in their boats. Some of the deadly metal devices account for 30 or 40 fish being retired by an unseen piling or stump.

Spinners, plugs, spoons, and bait are all used by the troller to entice salmon. The bright salmon encountered in a river's lower reaches are fresh and inclined to be somewhat more aggressive than those that have journeyed closer to the spawning grounds.

Spoons have their following also. Those equipped with a single siwash hook seem to hold the fish better than the treble.

A variety of plugs will give the angler an ample repertoire for all speeds of current and water conditions. Some plugs work best when pulled against the current while others have sufficient built-in action to wobble when the boat is moving downstream. The diving capability is not usually a big factor because the plug is held down by some kind of sinker.

Trolled herring catch a lot of salmon in fresh as well as salt water. This tempting morsel is presented in the round, plug-cut and spinner-cut.

TROLLING RIG

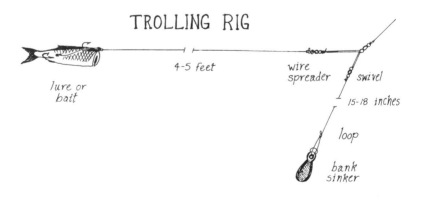

lure or bait

4-5 feet

wire spreader

swivel

15-18 inches

loop

bank sinker

HERRING HOOK UPS

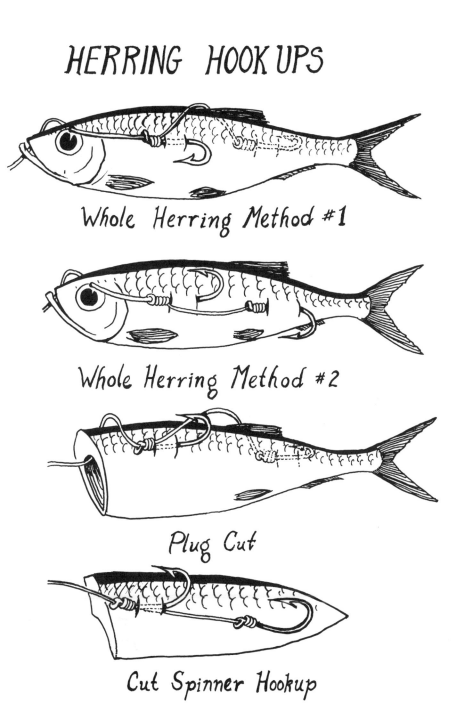

Whole Herring Method #1

Whole Herring Method #2

Plug Cut

Cut Spinner Hookup

A good basic way to rig for trolling is to tie the 17- or 20-pound main line to a wire spreader. The leader is 20- or 25-pound monofilament and should be 4 to 5 feet long. From the lower part of the spreader, 15 to 18 inches of fairly light monofilament is attached to the sinker. In the trolling process, the sinker is the most likely portion of the tackle to snag, so the monofilament attached to the sinker should be at least 5 pounds less breaking strength than the main line. A loop tied on the end of the dropper facilitates changing the bank sinker used in trolling.

A good rod choice for trolling is a Fenwick one-piece 1270-C. This stout rod is 7 feet long. A Penn 9 or 109 will hold sufficient line and gives reliable performance.

Water depths may vary from 5 to 15 feet. Since most of the fish are lying near the bottom and are unlikely to change their depth to pursue a lure, it is important to keep the offering at their level. The speed of the current and boat will also greatly affect the weight of lead used and amount of line paid out. A little experimentation and experience will be necessary to get everything working properly.

Begin by letting out line until the sinker is felt clunking the bottom. As soon as contact is felt, a couple of cranks on the reel handle will bring the lure to the salmon's depth. As the depth, current, or tide changes, the amount of line should be constantly adjusted. The lure should be reeled in every few minutes and cleared of any accumulated debris.

If the fishing is to continue for an extended period, use of a rod holder will eliminate arm fatigue. Something is lost, however, if the angler can't feel that first sharp strike as the salmon closes on the lure.

* * *

The eager morning crowd was already gathered as we arrived at the mouth of the Lewis. About 30 boats had formed a ragged hog line. Their close juxtaposition insured that any migrating salmon would have the opportunity of inspecting a plug or bait.

We joined the more aggressive boats that were trolling back and forth through the silty water. I had come equipped with two outfits. One rod was rigged with a Magnum Tadpolly for trolling upstream and the other with an easily-activated Kwikfish for the downstream leg.

Ron nosed the boat upstream and we let out the plugs. The right depth was reached and my rod went into the holder. My morning caffeine fit had been coming on for several minutes and the vacuum bottle was drawn. The steaming brew was barely poured when my throbbing rod arched. The scalding liquid seared my hands and filled my shoes as I lunged for the bucking rod. The uninspected drag was too tight and the wildly-thrashing salmon put so much pressure against the rod that it wouldn't come free from the holder's grasp.

Frantic pulling and jerking on my part finally freed the rod just as the line went slack. Ron found all of these antics highly amusing.

It took a few minutes to reorganize. My drag was properly

set, the plug went out, and my cup was refilled. The fish
seemed willing to allow me to leisurely sip my coffee. Several
spring chinook were hooked by neighboring anglers as our craft
weaved through the other trolling boats.

We were just settling into a nice rhythmical state of bliss
when my rod tip went down again. The action went as planned
and soon a sparkling 21-pounder was flopping on our floor-
boards. The first spring chinook of the year is always a special
prize.

Ron had his plug out first and was just fitting his handle
into the holder when he had a sharp strike. This fish was really
supercharged and spun off 50 yards of line before I could reel
in and help with the boat. The chinook charged right through
the middle of four boats but somehow Ron kept from tangling.
We followed out into the Columbia's mighty flow and chased
the fish for over half a mile before I was able to slip the net
under it.

To our amazement the tail hook on Ron's plug had skewered

the swivel attached to a huge Spin-N-Glo that was imbedded in the salmon's jaw. As soon as Ron released the tension on his line the hook slid out of the swivel. The fish had evidently been hooked by a bank plunker and broken off. As the plug wiggled by, the hook's point had found that tiny target and Ron had a free fish.

During all of this excitement the motor had died. As we made ready to head back upstream, the mouth of the Lewis looked a long way in the distance. Several pulls on the starting cord failed to produce the welcome explosion. A large freighter was proceeding up our side of the river at a good clip. Ron's expression of consternation turned to one of concern. He pulled harder and faster. We were on the edge of trouble. It's a bad feeling to be in the clutches of the Columbia's powerful current on a strong outgoing tide.

Finally, the stubborn engine turned over and we headed for the distant Lewis. The little outboard kept us barely ahead of the freighter. By the time we returned to the fishing grounds, the hot bite was over. Our plugs passed salmon with sealed lips for over an hour before we decided to call it a morning.

* * *

The black clouds hung low, ragged, and full of holes that cold April morning. Heavy rain pocked the otherwise smooth flow of the lower Willamette River. It was one of those mornings designed by Mother Nature to test the will and stamina of a salmon fisherman. Naturally, dozens of hopeful anglers were already trolling their offerings through the suspected lies of newly-arrived spring chinook.

In this type of weather the length of the fishing trip is in direct proportion to the amount of action observed or participated in. It's a rare fisherman who can truthfully say that he actually enjoys spending more than a few hours chugging through a bitterly cold rain when the fish are not biting.

We had been hard at it for three hours. Not a single shout from a surprised angler had been heard nor had we seen a net being clutched by a successful fisherman. The number of boats was rapidly diminishing. Those diehards remaining hunched deeper and deeper into their rain jackets.

The deluge's droplets trickled down my forearms everytime I raised my hands above the horizontal. Four layers of shirt and sweater sleeves were soaked to my elbows. The constant rain was beginning to dilute my enthusiasm.

The thought of a warm restaurant and a hot lunch became more and more pleasant and enticing. The recent run of fish must have passed and was probably finning by downtown Portland. My mind was forming the suggestion that we call it a day. Hopefully, rain-soaked Jerry would be as willing to depart as I.

Jerry's rod curved into a slow-motion arch. My first thought was that he had hooked the bottom. The adrenalin did not flow. His reel's clicker began a slow stutter. Our dulled senses gradually came alive. Only half believing, he wrenched the rod from its holder. A powerful surge nearly tore it from his cold, numbed grasp.

The heavy fish headed for the Columbia. A quick glance revealed only two other craft in sight. The battle would be fought without the usual necessity of weaving through the obstacle course created by a hundred trolling boats.

For a reason known only to the salmon, he reversed course and headed upstream. Jerry and I clumsily traded seats so that he could have both hands available to play the fish. Everything was under control. The fish's path brought him alongside. I grabbed the net and lunged at his head. The handle was a foot short and he swam away untouched. I had again forgotten to install the 8-foot handle designed to snare still-green salmon. As that white and tarnished silver form came by we could see he was well over 30 pounds. We also noted that both hooks had been buried in his mouth when the lunker had gobbled the trolled herring.

Our prospects of landing the salmon looked bright. The well-hooked fish headed upstream and would soon tire from the combined pressure of the current and Jerry's rod.

Around the bend through the downpour came a tug towing a raft of logs. The skipper was not about to change course or slow for some drenched salmon fishermen. Jerry pulled and cursed mightily as the big fish steered unerringly under the tug. The line grated and snapped and the only fish of the day continued its upstream journey to its manifest destiny. The tug's wake was almost too much for our little aluminum boat. A couple of gallons of froth slopped over the starboard bow. We rode out the waves on the wildly bucking craft.

The intruder passed and its wake was soon a rapidly fading scar on the dimpled surface. Our nerves settled as we silently communicated mutual thoughts. We headed for the warmth and succor of a nearby restaurant.

Back Trolling with Bait

Presenting a toothsome bait to the salmon with the aid of a diving device can be very rewarding. This technique allows the neophyte to effectively fish with very little previous training. The diver moves the bait very slowly near the bottom in a way that often proves irresistible to salmon.

The Hot-N-Tot plug was the original diving device used with this method. After removing the treble hooks, the plug is tied directly to the line. No sinker is involved. The leader will be 30 to 60 inches long and 15- to 25-pound test. Either two single hooks or a single and a trailing treble hold the bait. A small Spin-N-Glo adds a little visual attraction and helps impart natural buoyancy to the shrimp, prawn, herring or roe.

The diving device should be buoyant so that it will rise to the surface when not being pulled against the current. The Jet Planer was designed specifically for this type of fishing. This diver has three separate adjustments for various depths. At its deepest setting, it will fish at nearly 20 feet. Hot-N-Tots wiggle along at about 10 to 15 feet. No. 1 Hot Shots move the bait along at a depth of 10 to 12 feet. The diameter of the line is a considerable determinant as to the depth that the diver fishes. For best results the rod should be placed in a holder.

The boat is guided downstream in the same manner as used in plug fishing. The buoyant diver follows the river's currents and usually bounces off the numerous snags. Should its downstream progress be impeded, a little slack line will usually free it.

boat guided downstream

current ⟹

The initial take of the salmon can be a light tap. If there is a hint that a fish has the bait, the movement of the boat should be halted. The salmon will frequently mouth the offering before swallowing it firmly. When the fish really has the bait, the rod will be deeply bowed. When the rod goes down, the angler should set the hook hard.

Drift Fishing

Drift fishing for salmon is basically the same technique that has evolved for steelhead. Perhaps the biggest difference is the sometimes more pronounced strike of the salmon as compared to the frequently almost imperceptible take of the steelhead.

If boat fishing is possible, the fisherman will have much greater access to the fish. Whether to fish from an anchored boat or to free drift will depend somewhat on the size of the river, amount of traffic, and the craft's means of propulsion.

River Salmon Fishing

In a small stream the accepted technique is to fish from an anchored drift boat. In a larger river where most of the craft are power-driven, a boat anchored in the middle of a good hole will cause problems and hard feelings if the rest of the fishermen are moving over the holding water. Because of the power of some of the larger chinook, the odds of landing one are greatly increased if the angler can give chase with the aid of a boat.

When fishing from an anchored boat or from the bank, make the cast quartering upstream. The sinker should be in contact with the bottom by the time it is directly in front of the angler. The depth of the water and speed of the current will determine the angle and distance that the offering should be cast upstream.

Terminal Rig
for Drift Fishing

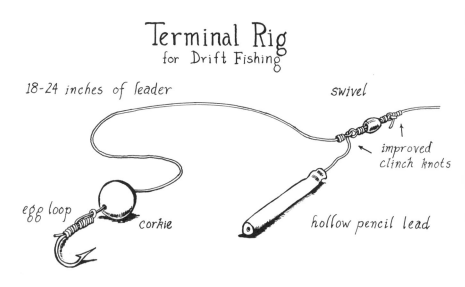

18-24 inches of leader

swivel

improved clinch knots

egg loop

corkie

hollow pencil lead

It is essential that the line be tight to the sinker. A bow in the line will make it difficult to control the drift and detect a strike. A straighter line will result from a sidearm cast than from an overhead one. A crank or two on the reel handle or a raising of the rod tip will remove the surplus line from the water.

If the sinker drifts over a deep pocket, bottom contact can again be made by free spooling some line or dipping the rod tip. The tight line will have a tendency to lift the sinker from the bottom at the end of the drift. A little free spooling as the drift is completed will prolong the sinker's contact with the bottom. Over-use of free spooling will result in an unwanted bow in the line.

An aggressive fisherman encounters some unusual conditions. One very productive fish-holding lie that I fish is blocked from normal methods by a cabin-size boulder. My technique here is to crowd up as close as possible to the downstream edge of this big rock and cast nearly straight upstream. The water is rather slow moving and even a light sinker fails to move unless given some assistance. As soon as the sinker clunks the smooth, rocky bottom, I begin to reel slowly. The pick-up is usually easily felt because of the tight line. Occasionally, however, the fish will drift downstream with the bait in its mouth, so it is necessary to be super alert.

Learning to detect that brief interval when the salmon has the bait in its mouth is a fine art. Honing this skill is the difference between catching a few hard strikers and putting many fish on the bank or in the boat. In the course of a drift, if the slightest twitch, tremble, breaking of rhythm, mushiness, unusual movement, tug or pressure occurs – strike fast!

When approaching a familiar drift, I always fish the best water first. After the known fish lies have been carefully plumbed, I probe the less promising areas. All too frequently an outside influence will arrive to spook the fish from the best spots that you have yet to try.

Unfamiliar pools can be explored from either the top or tailout. A careful covering of all the fishy looking water is in order.

Boondoggling

Drift fishing from an unanchored, moving boat is sometimes referred to as boondoggling. The technique is usually reserved for fishing large pools in big rivers where the fish are scattered. A minimum distrubance of the fish is achieved if the power boat skirts the holding areas when it moves to the top of the drift.

The cast is made in the desired direction and all slack is cranked in. Usually the boat will drift faster than the sinker and the lure will be pulled along the bottom. In large rivers the passing boat doesn't seem to disturb the bottom-hugging salmon.

If the waiting salmon elects to stop the lure, the take will be emphatic. If the salmon drifts downstream with the bait in its mouth, the angler will have to be very alert to determine that a fish is taking.

When tying the leaders used in bait fishing, an egg loop will help in securing the bait to the hook. The egg loop is tied like this:

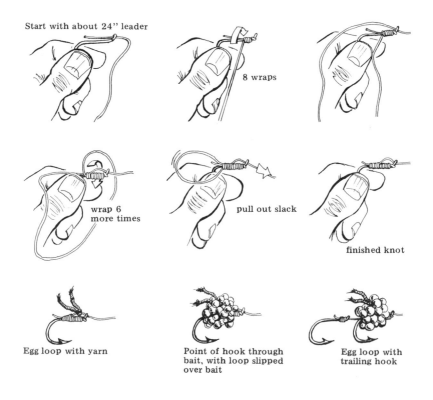

Start with about 24" leader

8 wraps

wrap 6 more times

pull out slack

finished knot

Egg loop with yarn

Point of hook through bait, with loop slipped over bait

Egg loop with trailing hook

METHODS FOR ATTACHING LEAD

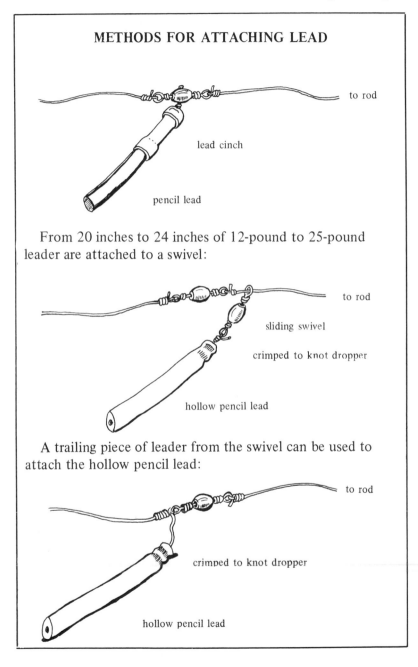

to rod

lead cinch

pencil lead

From 20 inches to 24 inches of 12-pound to 25-pound leader are attached to a swivel:

to rod

sliding swivel

crimped to knot dropper

hollow pencil lead

A trailing piece of leader from the swivel can be used to attach the hollow pencil lead:

to rod

crimped to knot dropper

hollow pencil lead

River Salmon Fishing

A strand or two of bright yarn is a definite asset in hooking the fish. As the lure is chewed, the yarn frequently catches on the salmon's teeth. The extra moment or so that the yarn holds the hook in the mouth gives the angler a little additional time to strike the fish.

* * *

My first encounter with a spring chinook came on an early April drift on the Kalama River. We were casting bobbers and eggs for steelhead and Walt managed to put a beautiful 8-pound spring fish in the boat from the very first pool.

An hour later we anchored in a deep, fishy run and began casting into the steamy water. My two partners were avid egg slingers and had discussed in great detail their "secret" egg recipes on the two-hour drive to the river. I had no doubt as to the effectiveness of the roe in many situations but had elected to fish a pink Spin-N-Glo.

My rhythmically bouncing sinker abruptly stopped and a sharp jolt bowed my rod. This was unlike any steelhead take that I had ever experienced. The fish majestically headed upstream with much authority. At about 75 yards it rolled heavily on the surface. It was obviously at least 30 pounds. The idea that anything except a steelhead had taken the lure had not occurred to us. One of my companions had raised the anchor and the other was pulling mightily on the oars in an attempt to chase the big fish. He expertly slipped the drift boat into the slack water on the side of the pool and after much exertion managed to reach the spot where the fish had rolled. I frantically cranked in the yielding line. The great fish revealed its broad purple back just off our bow. It was a big chinook. The approaching boat frightened him and he swam for the Kalama's headwaters.

There was much thrashing and grunting as the muscular oarsman tried to move the boat against the ever-increasing power of the current at the constricted throat of the pool. The fish never slowed when it entered the tumbling white water above the pool. The line melted from the spool when the rapids prevented any further upstream progress of the boat. When the moaning reel was nearly empty I clamped both thumbs on the spool and the 15-pound-test mono parted with a sickening twang. The salmon, not destined to satisfy an angler's ambition, continued upstream where he would shed himself of life for immortal reasons.

It took a few minutes for our dejected trio to recover. The oarsman's heroic efforts left him exhausted and we traded seats for the rest of the day.

Back Bouncing

The invention of the back bouncing technique greatly increased the efficiency of salmon fishermen who fish the strong currents of our larger rivers. The method is one of the most productive ways to fish for salmon. In addition, it makes it practical to fish some of the deep holes that are difficult, if not impossible, to probe by other methods.

Back bouncing consists of easing the boat slowly down the river and working the bait carefully along the bottom. In large rivers a motor is used to slow the downstream progress of the boat. In smaller streams oars hold the vessel back.

The critical part of the operation is to keep the sinker in contact with the bottom and slowly walking downstream. Different rates of flow and varying depths require constant change of sinker weight to insure the proper presentation of the bait. A certain rhythm and state of alert is required to detect the take as the salmon mouths the bait. A sensitive graphite or boron rod with a stiff tip greatly increases the ability of the angler to properly control the sinker and feel the salmon's take.

The rod should be sufficiently powerful to insure that 5 ounces of lead will not collapse the tip. The 7 1/2-foot rod blanks designed to be used as Flippin Stiks are ideal for this method of fishing. These blanks are made of graphite. The tip of the rod is continuously and somewhat rhythmically raised and lowered to assure that the sinker keeps moving.

Back bouncing on the Chetco River in southwestern Oregon. This method probably accounts for almost half of the fall run coastal chinook salmon taken along the Oregon Coast.

The casting reel is fished in free spool and line is paid out to keep the sinker in contact with the bottom. A tremble, twitch, hesitation, or jerk on the line indicates a fish may be mouthing the bait. After a large amount of line has been worked out, it will be difficult to control and feel the sinker. Reel in and start over.

River Salmon Fishing

Seventeen- or 20-pound-test main line works well. Since salmon don't appear to be leader shy, 20- or 25-pound monofilament is less likely to be frayed than lighter material by the salmon's sharp teeth. A pair of 2/0 or 3/0 hooks hold the bait. The lower hook snares many of the short biters. There are varying opinions as to the proper length of the leader. The original concept called for rather short leaders of 20 or 22 inches. Some feel that the thudding of the sinker bothers the salmon and opt for longer leaders of 30 to 36 inches.

Baits include herring, crawdad tails, salmon roe, ghost shrimp, and whole cooked or uncooked shrimp of the type found in the local fish market. Combinations of shrimp and roe are very popular.

The discovery that salmon would take ghost shrimp made procurement of bait much simpler. Salmon eggs are very expensive for those who don't fish the fall runs when the eggs are ripe.

A considerable industry for harvesting the shrimp from the Pacific's mud flats has blossomed along the coast. These little creatures range in size from 2 to 4 inches and vary in color from orange-red to whitish-yellow. A distinguishing feature is that one claw is larger than the other. Great efforts are made by fishermen to keep the shrimp alive and squirming. Ghost shrimp users immediately remove them from their marketing containers and spread them in a flat dish that has the bottom covered with paper toweling. It pays to be a little wary of the large pincers on the males. If they can fasten on your hands, blood blisters will result. Refrigeration is essential to keep the shrimp healthy.

The wings of a small Spin-N-Glo cause the lure's body to spin on the pivot of a fluorescent red bead and add some visual attraction as well as some buoyancy to the bait.

* * *

It was my first attempt at the newly-invented back-bouncing technique. A fishing friend had heard about it from a neighbor who had fished with an innovative guide who was one of the pioneers for the radical new method. The description of the tackle rigging was a little vague but we had the stiff rods and the proper double-hooked leaders rigged with Spin-N-Glos. We also had a generous supply of ghost shrimp and well-prepared salmon eggs.

When the kings (chinook) are in the Kenai River in Alaska becomes a very busy river.

There are several deep holes in the Cowlitz River where our regular methods didn't seem to work. These were selected for the test fishing. As we approached the first hole, our nerves tingled with excitement because we were armed with our newly acquired secret. Confidence and anticipation were extremely high as we let out our lines in the quiet gray overcast. Other salmon fishermen were on the river and they watched somewhat curiously as we steadily worked the bait through the deep water, raising and lowering our rod tips. For the first couple of hours we almost gloated because our expectation of success was so high.

River Salmon Fishing

After thoroughly probing three promising pools, a tinge of skepticism began to creep into my optimistic frame of mind. When one is fishing anadromous fish in a big river, unless he actually sees them rolling or cavorting on the surface, he never knows for certain if the quarry is actually present or is instead merely a phantasm.

Chris Bice cradles a three-year-old spring chinook from the Cowlitz River.

Two large salmon were landed almost simultaneously by nearby anglers pulling plugs. At least we knew that fish were in the river. My next inclination was to convert over to that proven technique. John eyed the glistening, netted fish with considerable longing.

We concluded that we must be doing something wrong. Our secretive informant had said to use bank sinkers weighing 2 to 4 ounces. We had decided to compromise at 3 ounces. As we neared the slow-moving, characterless tail-out, my line was almost straight up and down. Any salmon eyeing the offering would have to be almost under the propeller.

I reeled in and changed to 2 ounces of lead. The lighter offering bounced along several feet downstream of the boat. The slightest tremble came up the line to the graphite tip. I struck hard. The rod bucked. A 7-pound chinook rolled on the surface. The stiff rod quickly subdued his rushes and we had our first fish of the day. This little fish was more lustrous than silver and did much to renew our vigor.

We had a couple of cups of coffee and discussed the new fishing technique. John is a quick study and a very knowledgeable fisherman. It was decided that more attention should be given to the sinker since the whole object of the method is to present the bait near the bottom where the salmon lie.

We quickly motored back upstream to the deep, heavy water at the throat of the hole. The boat slid to a stop opposite a row of ancient battered pilings. John slipped on 5 ounces of lead and I 4. The boat hadn't backed down six feet when John reared back mightily and was into a good fish. The struggle carried us downstream a good quarter of a mile, where the beautiful 25-pounder reluctantly came to the net. The deep muscular body had the light-purplish cast of a spring chinook that has been in fresh water for a couple of weeks.

The sky brightened as the last of the clouds were carried away by the prevailing wind. Two more passes through the pool produced no more fish. Noon was almost upon us and we headed for the ramp. We chalked up the morning as a learning experience, a base of fishing knowledge on which to build.

Pulling Plugs

The concept of pulling plugs for salmonids originated in the
early sixties on Washington's Olympic Peninsula. Eddie
Pope had designed the Hot Shot with black bass in mind but
some innovative fishing guide conceived the idea of fishing the
plug downstream from his drift boat. Gentle, constant pulling
on the oars allowed the boat to slowly descend the river with
the plugs constantly working the water ahead. The steady, throbbing wiggle of the Hot Shots agitated or excited the steelhead
into striking. Fishing the plugs at the proper pace developed
into a fine art with the guides. They usually reserved the technique for the dudes who couldn't cast or drift fish. However,
even with expert fishermen in the boat, there are fishless periods.
When this unpleasantness occurred, the deadly plugs would
come out in midafternoon in order to prevent the dreaded
"skunk" day.

Chetco River guide Val Perry nets a fall chinook. Jack Hanson photo

Before long it became apparent that salmon would also hit
the plugs. In certain types of water, salmon would mouth the
plugs at least on a par with other fishing methods and lures.

Gradually the Hot Shots' reputation as a fish catcher ex-
panded and within a few years the lure was widely used for
both salmon and steelhead.

On a visit to California I had the opportunity to tour the Eddie Pope Company and was able to observe the manufacturing process of these increasingly famous Hot Shots.

The last step before the lure went into the packaging department consisted of the plug being placed on a special jig to insure that the screw eyes and hooks were in correct alignment with the body of the plug. One woman had been sitting at the same position in the assembly line for several years and she quickly made adjustments with a pair of needle-nose pliers.

I was amazed that about every fiftieth plug that came off the assembly line was actually pulled through a long tank of water to observe if it was running properly. If the plug was not swimming straight, some fine-tuning was done to the manufacturing process.

The Eddie Pope Company was eventually sold but the Hot Shot lure survived. Because of modern-day automation, current Hot Shots and most other plugs need to be tuned by hand. When putting a new plug into the water, the fisherman is advised to determine if it is running straight. A slight bending of the eyelet where the line is attached will straighten a wandering plug. Hold the plug's nose toward your nose. If the plug runs off to the left, bend the eyelet slightly to the right. A right running plug should have its eyelet bent to the left.

Some plugs have almost magical qualities about them. For mysterious reasons two seemingly identical plugs can be run side by side and one will receive more strikes than the other. I have a habit of scratching a mark on the nose of a plug when it catches a fish. A plug that accounts for three fish begins to be treated with a certain reverence. A six-fish plug rates a separate zip-lip envelope, and a protective attitude.

Shortly before writing this, I snagged and lost a Magnum Tadpolly that had accounted for nine spring chinook. No amount of manipulating and tugging the line would release the piling's hold on the treble and finally with great reluctance I snapped the line.

River Salmon Fishing

* * *

The first time that I tried pulling plugs in the mighty Cowlitz River from my drift boat my arms became weary
from holding the boat back against the heavy current. Rowing
in a big, powerful river is considerably different than in the
more gentle flows of rivers like the Bogachiel or Kalama. On
my next trip I used an outboard motor and the salmon didn't
seem to mind a bit.

Care should be taken to select the correct size line when fishing plugs. If the line is too light, the salmon will snap it off on
the strike. Many times an 8- or 10-pound-test has been broken
as the rod arched down under the attack of a heavy fish. When
I went to 20-pound it was soon discovered that the larger diameter prevented the plug from diving to its maximum depth.
A good compromise would be 12-to 15-pound-test.

The constant pulsating of the plug will tend to cause some
wear on the line where it knots to the eyelet. It is good insurance to reknot every couple of hours even though no fish has
been encountered.

Some plug fishermen like to use fluorescent line. The highly
visible monofilament makes it easy to keep track of the exact
location of the plug as it works it way down the river. Experienced plug pullers who know the traditional fish lies can put
their lures right on the noses of the holding salmon.

There is some controversy as to whether the fish can also see
the bright line. Many believe that the fluorescence will frighten
some of the more timid fish. Fluorescent line doesn't seem to
alarm the fish in rivers that are clouded by glacial silt. It is not
a bad idea, when using fluorescent line, to tie into a strong barrel swivel. Use about 5 feet of clear or camouflage line between
the swivel and the plug. The swivel will also help to keep weeds
and other debris from collecting on the plug.

Most manufacturers will be very explicit on their instruction
sheet as to whether a snap swivel or just a snap should be used
for attaching their particular plug. Their experience and test-
ing have proven which fastening technique will best enhance
their plug's action.

I like a high quality graphite rod with a light tip but powerful butt for pulling plugs. My favorite is an 8 1/2-foot Lamiglas G1310T. After a little experience, the fisherman will know the proper cadence imparted to the pulsating tip by each plug's action. Any change in the beat can indicate a hit, snag, weeds, or too fast or too slow movement of the boat. The alert skipper will quickly take action according to the situation.

Frank Amato tails a four-year old Clackamas River, Oregon chinook.

River Salmon Fishing

If the plug is specifically designed for salmon or steelhead fishing, the manufacturer will have installed hooks strong enough to hold these powerful fish. Some lures intended for black bass will also entice salmon to strike. These bass plugs usually come with flimsy hooks that will straighten during a battle with a heavy fish. It is a simple matter to change to 2X or 3X stout hooks.

As they come from the factory, most hooks will be fairly dull to very dull. A careful honing of the points is necessary to consistently hook salmon. A salmon has a very tough, bony mouth. It is actually possible for a salmon to close its mouth on a dull-hooked plug and eject it without ever being hooked. Needle-sharp hooks are much more likely to catch a rough spot in the mouth and begin the necessary penetration beyond the barb.

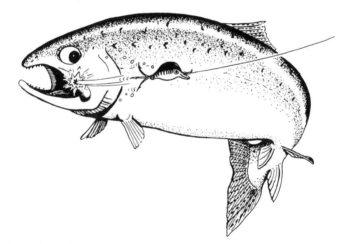

Straight-pointed trebles seem to hook better than the turned-in point types. Straight-pointed hooks should be filed on two sides so that the point has a triangular shape.

One other weak link that commonly occurs in plugs is the split ring that attaches the hook to the eyelet. If these rings are made of brass, they will probably fail under stress of a large fish. Brass split rings should be replaced by those made of stainless steel.

Some areas have banned the use of treble hooks in order to facilitate the release of fish. Trebles can easily be replaced by single siwash hooks. Some consideration should be given to the size and weight of the hooks when this is done because the responsible manufacturer has very carefully selected a hook of a size and weight that will effectively bring out the potential of its plug's action. An ammunition reloading scale is a great aid in cross referencing the weight of single hooks with trebles.

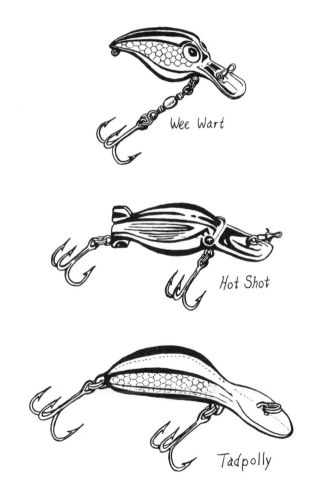

Wee Wart

Hot Shot

Tadpolly

River Salmon Fishing

The depth and power of the water to be fished plays a major role in the selection of the plug since they dig to widely varying levels. With the usual 45 or 50 feet of 12- or 15-pound-test line paid out and with no additional weight attached, a No. 3 Hot Shot will fish at a depth of 7 to 8 feet. A regular-size Tadpolly will cruise at 9 or 10 feet. Wiggle Warts and Wee Warts descend to 10 or 11 feet. A No. 25 Hot Shot will go down to about 12 feet. Probably the deepest runner is the Hot-N-Tot which will dive close to 15 feet. These depths are all approximate and will be affected by the diameter of the line and the power of the current.

To begin fishing a pool with plugs, position the boat directly above the suspected holding water of the salmon and keep it steady. In the average situation each fisherman lets out 45 or 50 feet of line. The plugs fish most efficiently if all fishermen spool out the same length of line. In tight circumstances it may be necessary to use shorter lines.

As soon as the proper amount of line is released, the boat operator starts pulling on the oars or adjusts the motor's speed to allow the boat to barely slide downstream. If the holding area is wide and the boatman is rowing, a zig zag course down the river will effectively cover most of the water. If a motor is used, a straight course is usually followed because the motor allows several runs through the pool.

The safest procedure is to fish with the rods in pole holders. Sometimes, the salmon will tap the plug a couple of times before solidly taking it. It takes rigid discipline to resist jerking the rod in response to a fish's tentative tap. When the salmon really has the plug, the rod will bow in a deep arch. The angler should strike hard. Immediately after the fish is solidly hooked, the pressure should be relaxed a little or the line will be snapped. Sometimes the uninitiated will clamp down on the spinning spool with both thumbs and the powerful fish will break the tackle.

It is also possible to anchor above the suspected holding water, place the reel in free spool and release a few inches of

line at a time. This technique slowly eases the plug down the drift without losing position. After the plug is reeled in, the rod tip can be moved a few feet and the procedure repeated.

When the salmon is in the net and if it is to be kept, it should be dispatched with the fish billy before the hooks are removed. The dangling trebles can be very hazardous to the fisherman.

* * *

The spring chinook were very aggressive and cooperative that beautiful sunny morning on the Cowlitz and we already had three lunkers in the boat. Our sensitive rod tips pulsated as the diving plugs probed the depths of the holding water just below the Barrier Dam. My tip dipped slightly and then curved almost to the surface. The fish proved to be a dark 6- or 7-pound chinook jack that appeared to have been in the river a long time. Compared to the three clean, bright fish in the box, he looked undesireable. I decided to release him.

A quick search failed to reveal the needle-nose pliers that we used to extract hooks. My fishing partner, Walt, was busy untangling his line and swore he wasn't sitting on them. The fish seemed docile enough and I decided to pull out the hook with my fingers. As the imbedded hook cleared his gums, he gave a mighty twist and the second dangling treble became deeply implanted in the joint of my left thumb. Over the years a few fish hooks had punctured my hide but none like this. We found the misplaced pliers and I began to pull and twist on the deeply set hook. It was into the joint well past the barb. I asked Walt to give it a try. He looked the other way and suggested that this was a job for a doctor.

The bite was hot and I hated to leave but the thumb was beginning to smart. We decided that Walt would stay with the boat and I would drive myself to the doctor.

As I pulled into the gas station in nearby Salkum, the smiling proprietor walked up to my open window and I asked the location of the nearest doctor. He inquired about my malady and I held up my throbbing hand decorated with the dangling Tadpolly. He turned a little green and looked away. He mumbled something about a doctor in Mossyrock, ten miles up the road.

Mossyrock proved to be a very small town and the doctor's office was quickly located. The nurse started asking the usual probing questions to which a new patient is subjected. A voice from the inner office questioned her about the affliction and she replied that there was a man with a fish hook in his thumb. The voice said that he had extracted dozens of fish hooks over the years and not to worry. We continued with the forms until the doctor appeared. He was well into his eighties, maybe even ninety. My confidence ebbed when I noticed his hands shaking from a severe case of palsy. He looked at the injured thumb and casually mentioned that he had never seen one quite that bad. The knot in my stomach twisted tighter. He asked if I'd had a tetanus shot lately. The last one that I could recall was administered many years earlier while I was in the Navy. He cited various statistics about how many people had died the year before from tetanus and instructed the nurse to inject me. She also daubed a little alcohol on the wounded thumb.

The ancient doctor picked up a mean looking scalpel with the palsied hand and prepared to make an incision. I almost

lost my nerve. Miraculously, his hand steadied as the knife
neared the hook and a deft slice freed the offending point. My
sigh of relief must have been audible all the way back to Salkum.

He skillfully placed an elaborate bandage on the repaired hand.
The gleaming plug was admired by both the good doctor and his
amiable nurse. He looked around for a container and finding
none decided to wrap it in a bandage to insure that the sharp
hooks would not repuncture me. He stuffed the bandaged plug
into my shirt pocket and sent me on my way.

Twenty minutes later I was back on the banks of the Cowlitz.
Walt beached the boat and queried about my injury. I held up
the bandaged hand with the thumb concealed by the outstretched
fingers. "Looks like he had to amputate," said I.

Since I had pulled several practical jokes on Walt over the years
he was a little suspicious. I reached in the pocket with the other
hand and pulled out the thumb-sized bandaged plug and held it
up for inspection. "There it is," was my casual comment. Walt
turned green and sank to his knees. He looked like he was going
to get sick. I managed a straight face for a good 30 seconds while
Walt fought for control. Finally, he detected a lack of proper
suffering on my part and leaped off the rocks and seized my
bandaged hand. We had a good laugh and went back to fishing.

River Salmon Fishing

* * *

Charlie had never caught a chinook and was super excited as we unloaded his cartopper at the Cowlitz's uppermost ramp. The eastern sky was barely pink as the peeking sun hinted that this was going to be a beautiful day. We were the first arrivals on that fine spring morning. A quick glance at my water level marker indicated that the dam was releasing a less than average flow of water.

We snapped on Hot Shots. Charlie was going to use a red and white, which he had selected from my teeming tackle box. My choice was a silver and blue.

Alaskan Guide Herb Good (right) and assistant Pee Wee Parker hold 81-pound chinook salmon (king) caught in Alaska's Kenai River.

We cruised out into the steaming current right into a hot bite. Charlie's wiggling plug had barely dug to the bottom when his rod bowed into the water past the second guide. I had forgotten to check the drag tension on his reel. The newly spooled monofilament held and he desperately struggled to wrench the bucking rod from the clutch of the holder. With a joint effort we managed to clear the rod from the hold of the unyielding tube, loosened the drag, and gained some semblance of control over the cavorting fish. The little round-bottom craft was nearly capsized in the process.

The heavy fish wallowed on the surface. It looked a solid 30 pounds. I didn't see how it was going to be possible to run Charlie's motor and net the big fish at the same time. After a quick conference we decided to beach the tippy boat on the opposite bank and land the hefty fish from solid ground.

As I nudged the bow onto the gently sloping gravel, Charlie hopped out while holding the rod high above his head. The fellow was surprisingly agile. I killed the engine, threw out the anchor, grabbed the net and was in hot pursuit as Charlie stumbled along over the slippery stones. Several hundred yards downstream the glinting lunker eventually tired and seemed ready to surrender. I waded to the top of my boots as eager Charlie horsed the almost spent fish toward the outstretched net. "A little closer," I urged. The current of the powerful river held the exhausted fish just beyond my reach. I stretched as far as possible, lunged at the fish, and was two inches short.

The fish seemed to yawn and the plug floated free. The chinook slowly sank from sight. This was the heaviest fish that had struck this season. Charlie took it pretty well. No loud cursing or gnashing of teeth, just a slight hang-dog look around his mouth. I muttered something unconvincing about there being plenty more fish in the river.

As we got back into the boat, I noticed that there was a big chunk of plastic broken off the bill of Charlie's plug. I suggested that he replace it with an intact version but Charlie firmly refused.

River Salmon Fishing

We eased out into the rushing current and let out the vibrating plugs. This time Charlie checked his drag tension. The rods went into their holders. I made a comment to the effect that if that broken plug didn't catch a fish in short order that it should be replaced.

Down went Charlie's tip again. The keen fellow was a fast learner and dextrously retrieved his rod, set the hook, and began to fight the fish. This one was even bigger than the first. We chased the tough chinook better than a quarter of a mile downstream before it began to tire. It looked like netting time was near and we again decided to beach the little boat.

As I crunched the bow into the shore's rocks, Charlie nimbly jumped out. The big fish was soon finished. I waded in and sank the net under him and we struggled ashore. It was nearly 40 pounds. Charlie laid his rod on the stones and walked up to the top of the bank. He looked up at the multi-tinted sky with his back toward me. For a long time he stood there without moving. I dispatched the fish with a rock. Charlie remained motionless. The hooks were removed. Charlie eventually came down and sat by the gleaming fish. His hand stroked the purplish back. He had a strange look on his face. Neither of us had said

80

a word. No yelling. No hollering. No smile. I thought of a story I had read recently of how the ancient Indians held the majestic chinook in reverence.

Charlie picked up the fish with his trembling hands and gently said, "thanks."

Drift Fishing With A Cork

Fishing chinook and coho with a cork has been a proven technique for many years. The method is very effective in snag-filled, slow-moving pools or in tide water where regular drift fishing results in hung sinkers. The secret to cork fishing is knowledge of the depth of the water and adjusting the length of line from the cork to the sinker to insure that the bait is drifting at the same depth as the fish are travelling or holding. Trial and error or keen observation of fellow fishermen is required to learn the migratory paths of ascending salmon.

To rig for this type of fishing a cork and then a barrel sinker are threaded on the line. The line is then tied to a size 7 barrel swivel. Both the cork and sinker are allowed to freely slide on the line. Above the cork a piece of rubber band is knotted to prevent the upward movement of the cork. The rubber band is easily moved up and down the line to adjust for various depths of water and will readily slide through the rod guides.

A 2-foot leader is tied to the other ring of the barrel swivel. Favored baits are salmon eggs, crawfish tails, and ghost shrimp. The weight of the sinker should be balanced to that of the cork so that it won't sink it, but at the same time be heavy enough to carry the bait near the bottom. The size of the cork and sinker are coordinated according to the type of water being fished.

The take of a cork-suspended bait can vary between a subtle

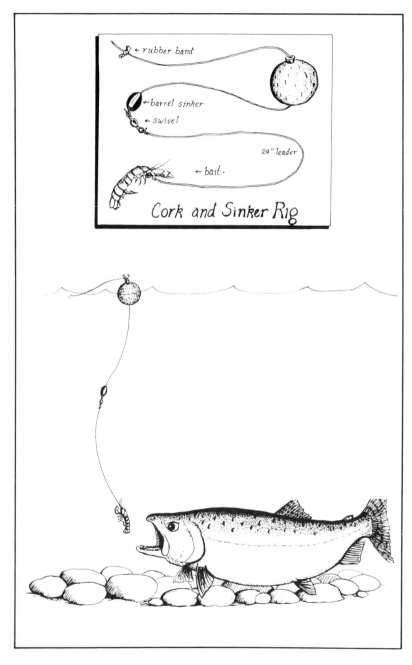

twitch to a dramatic, sudden total disappearance of the float. Sometimes the cork will skitter crazily cross or up current. It pays to keep your eyes riveted on the cork. The take lasts for only a brief moment.

* * *

On a late fall morning I was standing at the tailout of a long pool fishing for early arriving winter steelhead. The fish gods had been generous and a glistening 9-pounder lay on the bank near my feet.

A 30-foot cliff restricted my fishing efforts to about a 60-foot stretch of very quick water on my side of the river. It was a beautiful steelhead lie and my casting had produced several fish from this run over the years.

A fellow noisily crashed through the brush on the other side of the pool and planted his boots on the edge of a slowly revolving eddy about 50 yards upstream. The thick brush normally kept anyone from fishing his side of the river.

I noticed that he had a large cork on his line and quickly categorized him as a Canadian steelheader. He evidently had some good local knowledge of the river because within five minutes his rod was bent over to the water. A fresh coho went zinging down the pool and danced over the rippling surface before my startled eyes. The angler had great difficulty with his rod catching in the bushes but his stubborn efforts finally brought the acrobatic fish to his feet.

I kept casting to the steelhead water and watched him hook six more coho from his eddy in the next hour.

On my next visit to the river I was armed with corks and eggs. When I crossed the bridge and drove down the narrow gravel road toward the location of the pool, I was stopped by a gate and several No Trespassing signs. If coho were still present, they were not disturbed by me.

Plunking

Plunking appeals to the fisherman who is out for a relaxing experience in the fresh air. Areas on a river's course that have a reputation of producing fish for the plunking clan will be heavily populated with folks looking for a salmon dinner.

In those channels where salmon migrate close enough to shore to be in casting range of a heavy surf or spinning outfit, the plunker has a good chance of intercepting a passing fish. The method is relatively uncomplicated. The main secret is to place the appealing offering in the migratory path of the up-stream moving fish. If the bait or lure happens to tickle some instinct or curiosity of the salmon, some action is likely to ensue.

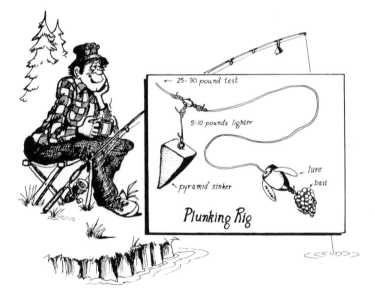

Patience and a laid back attitude are absolutely necessary since several fishing days are sometimes required to come up with a strike. On a few rare occasions the fish gods will bring a horde of eager biters into a river and the lucky plunker will be blessed with several strikes in a matter of hours.

The traditional rigging for plunking is a long, heavy rod, large-capacity reel, and 25- or 30-pound monofilament. The line is attached to a 3-way swivel. A dropper is run to a pyramid sinker of sufficient weight to hold the lure or bait stationary near the bottom. The dropper mono is 5 or 10 pounds lighter test than the main line to insure ease of breaking in case the sinker becomes fouled on a snag.

The leader is attached to the other ring of the 3-way swivel. Salmon eggs, shrimp, prawns and herring are all used for plunking. Even more popular are lures such as Spin-N-Glos, Glo-Gos, Kwikfish, and spinners. Sometimes the lure's hooks are tipped with salmon eggs. The length of the leader is determined by trial and error and depends on the buoyancy of the offering, depth of water, and power of the current. About 3 feet of monofilament would be a good starting point.

Salmon are unlikely to take any lure below their depth. Because of this trait the lure should be at or slightly above the depth at which they are migrating.

Since the plunker's attention may wander after awhile, a small bell is usually placed near the tip top of the rod. The jerk of the salmon and resulting titillating tinkle will quickly catch the lagging attention of all fishermen within earshot. A mad scramble to the gyrating rod will be necessary to securely implant the munched hook before the salmon departs.

Hog Line

Plunking from a boat is usually referred to as fishing from a hog line. The method is similar except that an anchored boat is used to position the plunker over the salmon's migration path. Because casting isn't necessary, much shorter rods are employed.

Some consideration should be given to the relationship of the leader's length to that of the rod when rigging. When a fish

River Salmon Fishing

is being landed, the 3-way swivel will not pass through the rod's tip top. A very short rod fished with a long leader will make it difficult for the angler to lift the fish high enough to be netted.

A spring chinook hogline scene on a tributary of the lower Columbia River.

A couple of years ago at the mouth of the Lewis we watched two frustrated hog liners try time after time to bring a big, sullen spring chinook to the net. One fellow was using a rod barely 5 feet long. For some reason he had attached a 7- or 8-foot leader to his plug. We never saw the fish but judging from the degree of bend in the stubby rod, it must have been a big one. The net-wielding partner was a heroic type and dug the net into the chilly water well past his elbows. He still couldn't reach it. In frustration he grabbed the leader with his hands. It snapped and both the plug and fish were gone.

When a hog liner hooks a fish it is frequently necessary to give chase when the salmon makes a freedom-seeking downstream run. A buoy attached to the anchor line enables a very rapid departure. Besides, the hot spot will still be available after the fight is concluded. Accepted procedure is for the boat to return to the anchor buoy, tie up, and resume fishing.

Fly Fishing

Fly fishing is actually one of the most effective methods of angling for various salmons. Its major limitation is the difficulty of presenting the fly at the fish's eye level when they are lying in deep, cold, powerful currents. There are lots of exceptions but generally the fly should be presented near the bottom where the fish are holding. Salmon will take a fly on a dead drift. At other times they will be more receptive to one retrieved in jerks.

Fly — Sockeye

Sockeye are the most difficult to entice to take. This species feeds on tiny plankton and is the least aggressive of the salmons in fresh water. In Alaska, where they migrate into the rivers by the millions, most of the reds that are fair-hooked in the mouth have struck a fly.

Before the Alaskans became conservation-minded, most reds were snagged by heavy spoons or jigs decorated with treble hooks. Enterprising fly fishermen discovered that the scrappy sockeye in the Russian and Moose rivers would strike bright bucktails. Treble hooks are now outlawed and fly fishing prevails in these rivers. The crowds of fish and fishermen are incredible.

The regulations in these rivers allow the fly to be propelled with a spinning rod and weighted with a sinker. The fishermen are so numerous that conventional fly fishing is usually very difficult. I made a visit to the Russian River with the intention of doing some fly casting for sockeye. The bank was lined with fishermen wielding spinning rods, and they were having great sport taking the fish with their gaudy bucktails. Many incredible tangles resulted when the acrobatic fish wrapped line around every accessible object, including competing anglers' legs.

Any attempt to fly fish would have resulted in my hooking a fellow human being on the back cast. I contented myself with watching the show and left after a couple of hours without wetting a line.

The more remote rivers in Alaska offer the opportunity to fly fish for the rambunctious reds. In their vast numbers an avid angler will find some biters that will open their mouths and inhale a fly. Frequently, a considerable number of casts are required to pinpoint a willing fish. Once hooked, fresh-run reds are very strong fighters and frequently clear the surface.

An 8-weight outfit is suitable tackle. These fish have the capability of making long runs and in open water can rip off many yards of backing.

Fly Knots

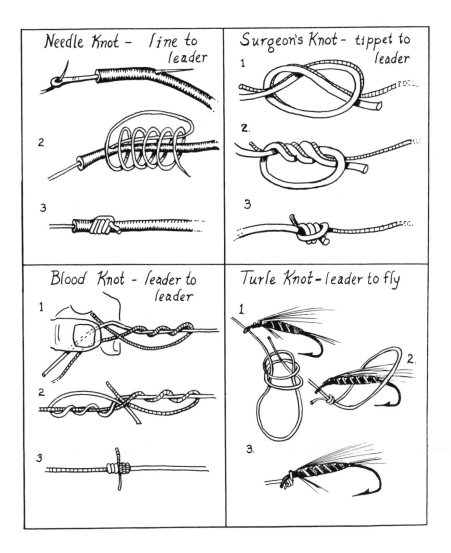

Needle Knot - line to leader

1

2

3

Surgeon's Knot - tippet to leader

1

2.

3

Blood Knot - leader to leader

1

2

3

Turle Knot - leader to fly

1.

2.

3.

Fly — Pink

The prolific pinks are very ready fly biters. Their relatively small size requires a light 6-weight outfit to allow them to demonstrate their full potential. They jump and cavort and make some reasonably strong runs.

One interesting fact about the fauna of the Aleutian's Adak Island is that there is no insect life, at least we never saw any. The combination of a fierce climate, lack of bushes and trees, and unrelenting wind precluded the survival of any bugs.

The pink run was on in force in the only readily accessible stream. Most of the fishing personnel of the naval base were crowded along Finger Creek's rocky banks during every break from their duties. The fishing was wonderful and rewarding for those who had never fished for salmon before and who were willing to endure the harsh elements.

Desiring a fishery offering less crowded conditions, I started perusing a detailed map of the island. A faint blue line on the Pacific side flowed into the sea about two miles from the base. Few of the personnel ventured more than a mile from the comparative civilization offered by the naval facility.

A couple of anglers gave me strange looks as I forded Finger Creek's misty mouth and headed along the rocky coast toward my desolate destination. Fifty feet into the tundra and there was no sign of another human being.

After a vigorous hour of trudging into the face of the island's typical 25-mile-an-hour wind, I reached the mouth of the remote stream. The only other inhabitants were a pair of stern bald eagles and a group of petulant Glaucous Gulls. Because I was anticipating the fishing of new water, the elements failed to evaporate my enthusiasm.

By good fortune, the wind lessened and the sky lightened. There was no blue, of course, but the overhead was bright enough to greatly raise my spirits.

As I assembled my fly rod, several shadowy gray blurs assembled at the meeting place of the stream's steady flow and the incoming tide. At this stage of my fishing career I had not yet become technically inclined or burdened with several fly lines and reels. The thought didn't occur that these salmon should be fished with a deeply sunken fly. It wouldn't have made much difference because my silk line had a habit of floating for about an hour and then becoming a slow sinker.

Group of happy fishermen -- Jim Teeny photo

My favorite bushy No. 8 Royal Coachman Bucktail was knotted to the leader. A few false casts and the fly was zipping over the growing school of gray forms.

The fly was allowed to drop on the slick above the white surge of the sea. Its surface dance was immediately interrupted by the deliberate head and tail rise of a 5-pound pink. The sting of the barb sent the silvery fish into a tail-walking display equal to the best efforts of a prime rainbow. The first frantic run stripped out most of my meager 25 yards of backing. Pinks are not usually the strongest of the salmons but this one put up about as energetic a battle as any 5-pound salmonid that I have ever encountered. The acrobatic display coupled with the beautiful surface take combined to achieve a memorable encounter. The gleaming fish came in after a few minutes. He was quickly dispatched and placed in my Trapper Nelson.

The drowned and chewed fly was replaced by a fresh version. The line was still buoyant but the fly was allowed to float into the sea without being munched by the gray shadows. Three casts later another pink decided to taste the strange looking floating object. The fight was not as determined as the first and a 4-pounder was quickly added to the Trapper Nelson.

The cycle was repeated twice more. Then, as though they had been waiting for a signal, all of the salmon in the tidal pool began to move upstream. Some mysterious phenomenon of nature released the spirit of the fish and they headed for their spawning grounds. They swam in their final bright stage of life slightly faster than I could negotiate the treacherous banks and were soon lost from sight.

The quirky wind reversed and quickened and blew and blew. Soon the grayish seascape wad dissolved by slanting rain. My step was heavy by the time I reached the waiting jeep in the deepening gloom of evening.

Fly — Chinook

Chinook are not the most aggressive of the salmons, but they will take flies if they are presented where they can see them.

When they are lying in deep flows, heavily-weighted lines and
flies will be necessary. Since these strong fish are capable of
pulling several hundred yards of line, a large-capacity reel with
a heavy-duty drag system is absolutely essential. A 10-weight
line and rod are required to handle the heavy flies and to stop
the powerful runs in a typical chinook fly fishing situation. A
detachable fighting butt will offer some welcome assistance
and leverage. Whereas the smaller species can be landed with
10- or 12-pound leaders, a 20-pound tippet of hard monofilament is not too heavy for a large chinook. Their teeth are very
abrasive and will wear through a leader during a long encounter.

Cam Sigler clutches a fly-caught spring chinook.

93

River Salmon Fishing

Two days of steady casting had failed to produce a rise on that fine crisp September weekend on the Deschutes. I had been through my entire repertoire of favorite steelhead patterns and had finally returned to the proven No. 4 Green Butt Skunk.

Donna Teeny tries to stop the powerful run of a large spring chinook.

Steelhead seemed to be scarce or reluctant and the chilling wind was tying knots in my leader and dissipating my fishing ambition. The decision was made to give it another five minutes before departing for the solace of camp and a cup of scalding coffee.

With this promise of comfort in mind, I returned to a state of ready alert and watched the tip of the highly visible line guide the fly over an inviting slick caused by one of the river-bed's numerous sunken boulders. The faint coppery glow of the beginning sunset outlined the wake of the swinging fly.

A large fish, released from the glare and fear of the day, took with an explosive boil the size of a wheelbarrow. Naturally, I thought that this was a heavyweight steelhead.

The powerful fish turned expertly into the main current and headed for the sanctuary of the distant Columbia. Five-hundred stumbling yards downstream and twenty knuckle-busting minutes later a summer chinook turned his flank of burnished silver at my feet and was tailed by my waiting hand. This was my first experience with a chinook making a surface rise. Lacking a scale, I did a quick taping job and recorded his length at 35 inches. He probably weighed 16 or 17 pounds. A rare surface-taking chinook, of course, could not be killed and was gently returned to the welcoming water in the hope that this unusual trait would be passed on to his progeny.

Since this phenomenon occurred four years ago, three more chinook have chosen to munch my fly as it coasted past, at or just beneath the surface.

Some of my best fly fishing for salmon actually occurred while I was casting for sea-run cutthroat trout. A favorite small river in western Washington boasts a salmon hatchery, and in the fall large numbers of chinook.

My plan was to walk along the clear flowing stream until I spotted a school of the highly visible chinook. Using my polaroids, I carefully examined the lower part of the pool; I would usually see several shadowy cutthroat waiting for chinook hens to drop their eggs.

The rowdy cutthroat would often speed the process up a bit and butt the bellies of the females, if no eggs were forthcoming without their assistance. When this happened, pandemonium would break loose in the pool as the protective males would chase the faster, cheeky cutts.

As soon as the pool calmed, the waiting cutts would readily attack any gaudy pattern presented to them.

The fish were within a few miles of the salt and all were in top condition.

River Salmon Fishing

Occasionally, a large chinook would open his mouth and yawn in my visible size 6 or 8 fly. I would enjoy a powerful run or two, possibly a wallowing leap, point the rod at the fish and break him off. As soon as my nerves settled, I would go back to the cutthroat. One day when the chinooks were particularly demonstrative, five salmon could be counted with my diminutive flies protruding from their massive jaws.

In this small stream it was virtually impossible to land a 30- or 35-pound chinook on my trout rod, but the big fish ignored any offerings presented on heavier salmon tackle. However, one evening when I was feeling particularly energetic, I decided to attempt a chinook capture using my trout outfit. My strategy was to put strong pressure on the first salmon hooked, chase it through the shallows, and exhaust it after a strenuous chase of several hundred yards. An 18-inch cutt postponed my plans a little when it took the No. 8 Spruce on the third cast.

After about 20 minutes a big male chinook mouthed the fly as it swam past his hooked kype. The hook was set but the bottom-hugging fish never moved. Pressure was applied until the 8-pound leader sang. The giant realized that something was wrong and shot to the head of the pool. He came back just as fast and headed for the salt. The little river was reasonably snag-free and with some heavy running through the shallows, I was able to keep up with the fish. Everything was going according to plan except that after several hundred yards the fish seemed as energetic and powerful as ever.

An unnoticed snag caught my foot as I plunged by and I fell face forward into a foot of water. As quickly as possible, I struggled to my feet. Unfortunately, about five gallons of water were scooped up by my unbelted waders. This dramatically impeded my progress. The big fish started to gain line as I staggered along with heavy legs. Drastic action was required if this fish was going to be landed. I wallowed up to a nearby gravel bar, laid down, and with a little grunting was able to raise my feet above my head. About half the water ran out of the waders. Inadvertently, the reel fell off the rod into the sand. Frantically, from the prone position, I tried to re-attach the reel.

The usually well-oiled mechanism made a horrible grinding whine and mercifully the leader parted.

After glancing around to see if there had been any witnesses to this debacle, I sheepishly emptied the rest of the water from my waders, wrapped the line around the frozen reel and headed for the car.

Fly — Coho

Silvers are great fly rod fish. They readily take a wide variety of feather, fur, and tinsel flies and when hooked stage a fast and usually acrobatic show. Fish, undisturbed by spoons or spinners, will sometimes come to the surface for rapidly stripped wet flies. Under certain conditions, coho will rise to large, bushy dry flies. One-hundred-fifty yards of backing is required to stop their energetic dashes. An 8-weight rod and line would be the right choice for these feisty fish.

Unlike most salmonids, the competitive coho sometimes becomes even more aggressive toward a fly when their pool is frothed by their wildly jumping hooked companions.

* * *

When I arrived at bleak Adak, several dozen flies of varying sizes were in my fly box. Steady fishing for pinks during the summer used up a lot of the flies. By fall, when the coho arrived, the inventory was pretty well depleted. A No. 10 Royal Coachman was the largest offering still available. The tiny hook seemed rather puny for the 10- to 15-pound fighters that were about to arrive.

At first, the quality of fishing depended entirely on the whims of the sea lions. Coho would stack up below a little falls, summoning up their strength to make the leap that would carry them over the obstruction to their spawning gravel.

The marauding lions would frequently swim the mile up the little river to the falls. After they had eaten their fill, they would take a bite out of each of the remaining trapped fish and leave them to die. During the night a new run would usually arrive. The Navy required that I keep irregular hours and on my first two visits to the falls only a few coho carcasses remained.

Fortunately for the fish and human fishermen, the marine patrols got into the habit of firing a few shots into the pool when the lions were present and the predators seemed less inclined to swim up the stream.

On my third visit, I was elated to see several dozen contented silvers lying in a loose formation spread over the entire pool. Some were suspended on the edges of the back eddies seemingly broadside to the thrust of the current. Others finned in the quick water, gliding past some jutting rocks just below the falls. Even in the dim light their flanks sparkled like the hue of new tin.

This was my first experience with a school of fish of this magnitude and my emotional state was well beyond mere excitement.

My fingers trembled as I knotted the diminutive No. 10 Royal Coachman to the 6-pound tippet. First I tried the fish holding below the falls. They ignored my efforts. A dozen fish, curious and alert, hung near the tailout. A sloppy cast slapped the water six feet in front of their holding position and sank to their level about three feet above the nearest waiting kype. Three hook-nosed beauties immediately darted at it. The fastest took the fly with a blurred flash and spectacularly cleared the water. His fright was transmitted to his companions and soon the whole pool was filled with flashing, racing fish. The coho was reluctant to leave and shot from the throat to tailout, time after time. Even with a body stored full of the sea's energy, he tired after a few minutes of violent runs and leaps. With awe and reverence, I lifted his sinewy, writhing form from the water and placed it on the gravel. The gleaming flanks approached the luminosity of pure silver. The tiny hook was deeply implanted in his vomer and by the time I worked it out the fly was pretty well tattered.

After a short rest, the scattered salmon settled in and the next cast produced another violent strike.

The fish were cooperative all morning. It mattered little that the hook was soon adorned by a few shredded remnants of the original dressing. It was with great reluctance that I departed for the next watch.

* * *

For several seasons I had fished British Columbia's beautiful Babine River for its October steelhead. The weather was frequently harsh and snow usually fell sometime during a week's fishing. The action was good enough to keep bringing us back for more.

Ejnar Madsen, the camp's owner, had casually mentioned on a previous visit that steelhead entered the river early in September. We decided to advance our timing by a month and arrived in mid-September with the hope of obtaining some warm weather angling.

Winter decided to arrive early that year and we were greeted by a three-inch soggy white covering the first evening after our arrival. Fortunately, our group was prepared for the severe conditions and we all had the necessary warm clothing.

The next day we fished some water below the camp and our party landed three coho in addition to several steelhead. These splendid salmon had a slightly bluish cast and were an unexpected bonus. Their muscular bodies seemed undiminished despite their several-hundred-mile journey from the sea.

That evening we were gathered in our cabin recounting the day's fishing and tying a few flies. Ejnar came in and asked if we would like to forsake the steelhead the next day and go up to his favorite pool for some coho fly fishing. This was a tough decision but the romance of unseen water was too much and the four of us decided to give it a try.

We asked Ejnar to recommend the best coho fly. "Very simple," said Ejnar in his Danish accent. "Just wrap a little red thread on the shank of the hook, tie in two grizzly hackle tips for the tail, and sparsely palmer a grizzly hackle to the eye of the hook." When Ejnar talked about flies, lures, or fish, everyone paid attention. The fly was quickly completed and held up for Ejnar's approval. "That's it!" was the reply.

"What do you call this creation?" was the next question. One of our party had placed bottles of McNaughton's and soda water on the table. As Ejnar's twinkling blue eyes coursed the room they riveted on the bottles. "Whiskey and Soda, of course!"

The next morning, armed with several Whiskey and Sodas, we piled into the camp's largest jet sled and headed for the coho hot spot. At the fish counting weir we changed to the big propeller-driven boat and began the journey to Smoke House Island. Here, the Indians cured thousands of sockeye for their winter's food. The bottom was strewn with carcasses of dead salmon. Lots of big rainbows dropped down out of Babine Lake to feed on the hundreds of millions of eggs deposited by spawning sockeye.

River Salmon Fishing

The rainbow grew so fat on the rich diet that they appeared almost grotesque. A 20-inch fish could weigh 5 pounds. They put up a heck of a fight even on our steelhead rods.

The island was also a favorite holding place for the later arriving cohos. We tried using the familiar dead drift technique that took the steelhead in the lower river.

Ejnar watched the non-productive effort for a few minutes and suggested that the fly be stripped in 6-inch pulls.

The change in technique produced a violent explosion within the first 20 feet. I was fishing a new 10½-foot Fenwick graphite and the long rod really received a workout. The fish was amazingly strong and after a few minutes of powerful runs and heavy surface swirls, I began to think I had tangled with a late-arriving chinook. During the next half hour, the dogged fish went deep into the backing on my St. John on four occasions.

Ejnar finally waded out to his boot tops and scooped up the big coho with the yawning net. The honest scale pulled down heavily. "How big, Ejnar?" "Twenty-two!" was the reply.

We had kept the salmon the day before for dinner and the big fish was slipped back into the water after the Whiskey and Soda fly was gently removed.

We had a little more snow but it only seemed to titillate the salmon's desire for the Whiskey and Soda. After perforating the lips of many salmon, we started the long boat ride back to camp. One of the group said he couldn't wait to get back to the cabin so he could make some more Whiskey and Sodas. We weren't exactly sure what he had in mind.

Fly — Chum

Pound for pound, chum are the strongest of the salmons. Also, when fresh from the sea, they are very aggressive toward flies. They make very powerful runs and can easily rip off a hundred yarns of backing. Fresh fish jump almost on a par with silvers and sockeye. An 8- or 9-weight rod and line are required to control these strong and active fish. The reel should be capable of holding 150 yards of backing. Since chum are the most likely of the salmons to hold in shallow water, they can frequently be taken with a floating line.

* * *

There was a light ripple on the dull uninteresting stretch of river that Bob had been referring to as Chum Flat. We had raced by several times in our quest for big summer chinook. A half dozen other boats had cruised down the main channel without stopping. Bob cut the engine and allowed the boat to drift. I climbed up on the bow of the sled, donned my polaroids, and looked carefully into the shallow water. There were thousands and thousands, acres and acres of chum salmon. This was the gathering place for chum before they began their swim up to their spawning grounds.

The newly arrived pods of fish were silvery bright and proud of their strength gleaned from the sea. They seemed to wait here until the greenish and pink splotches began to develop on their sides before moving upstream. We were just a few miles from Bristol Bay on the Alagnak River, well downstream from the upper limit of the tidal influence.

Bob allowed the boat to drift several hundred yards downstream until we were well past the hordes of fish. I was too awed to pick up my rod for a cast. Bob suggested that we catch a few and ran the boat back upstream and heaved in the anchor near a particularly heavy concentration of fish.

Alaskan angler Jim Repine with a calico salmon (also called chum or dog).

My heavy boron rod had been strung with a fast-sinking line. Trembling fingers managed to snip the fly and replace the spool with one filled with a 9-weight forward floater. Chum are particularly eager to crunch pink flies. A No. 2 streamer was clumsily knotted to a 15-pound tippet. It took a few minutes to calm down and get everything working right. On about the fifth cast I remembered to start twitching the fly on the retrieve. A response came in about three feet. A heavy swirl caused a large wave in the shallow water.

The lustrous fish made a short, forcible run and began a series of five surface-clearing leaps. Each successive jump was a little higher. The last was probably four feet and about as high as I have ever seen a salmon clear the surface. The drag chattered as the line splice rattled through the snake guides and the salmon ran deep into the backing. As soon as that long run was completed the fish frothed the surface of the shallow water as it tore around in a tight circle. The heavy tackle took its tool and the fish came to the boat in about ten minutes. The muscular specimen was fresh from the salt with only the faintest hint of the characteristic blotches that would develop as spawning neared. The barbless hook was easily removed without lifting the fish from the water.

Without moving the boat, we hooked at least 20 chum during the next couple of hours. The fresh, shallow-holding fish had a very strong inclination to jump.

During the superb week's fishing we left the chinook several times for the slam-bang sport offered by the forceful chums. When we fished for them several miles upstream, their spawning colors were very pronounced. They jumped less but were still extremely strong. As these fish ripen, they also develop an incredible and fearsome set of teeth. No way would an angler probe that terrible maw with his fingers to extract a hook.

Tackle Failures

Large salmon pull hard . . . very hard. They exert a terrific strain on every portion of the tackle and naturally any defect or weakness will result in an involuntary long line release.

River Salmon Fishing

During 30 years of pursuing salmon in our rivers, I've witnessed the hooking of several lunkers. The ones that escaped have often been more interesting than the ones which were captured. Both the successes and failures were entered in my Log Book and possibly a review of some of the failures will be helpful in preventing the loss of the trophy of a lifetime.

Despite the fact that the angler has armed himself with a high quality rod, reel, and premium line, there are lots of opportunities for tackle failure. Actually, most of the leviathans that I have seen lost came unbuttoned because something went wrong with the couple of feet of tackle next to the fish.

Lots of failures occur because of the hook and how it is attached to the leader. Hooks should be examined and snelled with warm hands and good light before leaving for the river. It doesn't make sense to spend valuable fishing time tying up leaders. It is not unusual to find a couple of defective hooks in a box of 100. Misshapen or rough hooks should be discarded. The fish catching ability of a hook is greatly enhanced if its point is carefully honed.

Some hooks are just too flimsy to land a large salmon. A simple test is to tie up a few leaders that you intend to use. Stick the hook's point into a solid object and pull. If the hook readily bends or breaks it has a good chance of failing when you try to stop that whopper from crossing the tailout into the rapids below.

Once the leaders are snelled, they should be safely stowed in a container that protects them from nicks, scrapes, and ultra-violet light. Once a leader has accounted for a fish, it should be retired. A salmon's teeth frequently fray a leader and a heavy strain over a considerable period may permanently weaken mono.

On three occasions I've seen cheap imported swivels break. Unfortunately, one was tied to the end of my line. A size 7 Rosco will probably hold any salmon but if you need even more confidence, try a size 5.

A lot of plugs and spoons come equipped with brass split rings. These are fine for bass but should be replaced with stainless steel if you expect to encounter a massive salmon.

The final few inches of line takes a severe beating from rocks and snags, and should be cut back every hour or two or after landing a fish.

Salmon eggs will eventually foul the reel's mechanism and impair its function. Reels should be cleaned and oiled periodically. After a few fishing trips, the amount of line broken off will make casting difficult and decrease the casting distance. Exposure to ultraviolet light will decrease the strength of monofilament. Reels should be kept full or nearly full of fresh, high quality line.

Rod guides can be broken or scored and wraps worn and frayed. Modern self-ferruled rods should occasionally have the male portion lubricated with paraffin. A brief insepction before departure will insure that the rod is functional and intact.

Care and Preparation

If a salmon is to be kept it should be killed with a sharp blow on the back of the head immediately after being landed. This is also the time to make the necessary entry on the Salmon Punch Card. The quality of the meat will be maintained if the fish is cleaned as soon as possible.

Cleaning is accomplished by inserting a sharp knife in the vent and slitting the belly to the gills and removing the entrails. A spoon is used to remove the dark, reddish-brown kidney line along the backbone. All parts of the gills should be cut out.

If immediate cleaning is not feasible, the fish should be placed out of the sun in the coolest available place. A damp burlap bag makes an excellent container. As soon as practical, the fish should be iced or refrigerated. A cleaned, refrigerated salmon will stay in top condition for three or four days. If it hasn't been devoured in that period of time, it should be frozen.

If we plan on baking or frying the fish sometime in the future, we remove the skin before freezing.

After the salmon is skinned, cut into serving size pieces and wrapped in freezer paper, place the pieces in an air-tight Tupperware container. These frozen fillets will stay in excellent condition for several weeks. The wrapped, frozen pieces do not stick together and they can be removed from the plastic dish as needed.

Recipes

If a complex gourmet salmon recipe is desired, I would suggest the fine books on fish cookery by James Beard and Jane Hibler. My wife is a gourmet cook and uses all of the known aids and condiments when she cooks these splendid fish. When it's my turn to prepare the salmon, I use only the simplest methods to complete the job. I justify my uncomplicated procedures by referring to the natural, fine flavor already present in this toothsome delight.

Jerry Siem with a newly-arrived silver.

Probably the simplest and most popular method is barbequing with a covered barbeque grill. The salmon is cleaned. Head, tail, and fins are cut off and the bones are removed with a fillet knife. If the fish is fresh, the skin is left on and the fillet is placed directly on the metal grate. If the salmon has been frozen, the skin may impart a slightly fishy flavor to the meat. This isn't necessarily bad and skinning is a matter of personal preference. If the fillet is skinned, it should be placed on a layer of aluminum foil rather than directly on the grill. If the particular fish has a high oil content, no additional oil is necessary. If a higher degree of oil is desired, the fillet may be brushed with melted butter or safflower oil, depending on your desired cholesterol intake.

Seasonings are a matter of personal preference. My own choice is freshly ground black pepper and diced onion. A little garlic powder adds a nice touch.

When some variety is desired, we coat the whole fillet with green goddess salad dressing. When this is done, no other seasonings are necessary. Cooking time over a medium covered fire is between 45 and 75 minutes depending upon the thickness of the meat.

Several years ago I was watching the Lucky Jim Show on television and Jim Conway revealed one of his secrets for barbequing fish. When he had the fire burning really hot, he stripped some leaves from a nearby red alder tree and threw a couple of large handfuls on the coals. Large bellows of smoke resulted and he quickly covered the grill so the fish would soak up the smoke. The way his guests went after the alder-flavored fish left no doubt as to its succulence.

The next time we had barbequed salmon I gave it a try.

The alder is considered a weed tree west of the Cascades and the leaves are readily available. We have several in the yard. The leaves give the fish a marvelous smoky flavor to which I have become slightly addicted.

Most Americans and Canadians have enjoyed the delights of a fish and chips meal. The eating quality depends on the variety and freshness of the fish used. Anyone fond of fish prepared in this manner will go wild over recently caught salmon cooked in the following way.

Deep Fried Salmon

The salmon is filleted and the skin is removed. I usually save the belly walls of the fish for this method. Cut the fish into strips or squares, being sure no piece is over an inch thick.

Three bowls are required. In the first, place a generous amount of whole wheat flour sprinkled with pepper and any other seasonings that titillate your palate. Break three eggs in the second bowl and add a cup of milk. Beat together.

Run a few slices of whole wheat bread through the food processor and place the resulting bread crumbs in bowl number three. Commercially-prepared bread crumbs may be substituted if desired.

Roll the salmon pieces in the first bowl. Dunk into the second bowl, press into the third bowl.

Jim Teeny displays a world-record humpy.

River Salmon Fishing

Half fill a metal sauce pan with safflower or corn oil and bring to a high heat. Place the breaded fish in a deep fry basket and insert into the hot oil. Cook until golden or medium brown. If a fry basket is not available, simply place the breaded pieces in the hot oil and remove with a slotted spoon when cooked.

Donna Teeny about to release a beautiful chrome sockeye.

Deep frying is normally associated with high cholesterol. This recipe uses mostly low cholesterol ingredients. If it is necessary to keep cholesterol and/or caloric intake at an absolute minimum, roll the salmon in the whole wheat flour and skip bowls two and three.

Smoked Salmon

For years I prepared the brine for smoking salmon in a haphazard fashion. Into any available container went a handful of salt and another of brown sugar. This was dissolved with a random draught of water drawn from the tap. Sometimes the results were fairly palatable but too frequently the results ended up being mixed with the dog's food. At times the dog seemed pleased with the arrangement but occasionally he walked away in apparent disgust.

Obviously, something had to be done because some mighty fine fish was being wasted. I read a couple of books on the subject and discussed the matter with local experts. The problem with the local experts was that they had constructed elaborate smoke houses or utilized unsightly ancient converted refrigerators that detracted from the beauty of the landscape. Some of the more industrious spent days preparing the fish and tending the fire. Much of the time the finished product was truly excellent.

Unfortunately, I had neither the desire to build a smoke house nor the time and patience to tend a fire for an extended period. If you are of similar inclination, the following method and brine recipe will produce excellent results.

First, it is necessary to obtain a Luhr Jensen Little Chief Smoker. If you must keep the box, use it only for storage. The beauty of the Little Chief is that the heating unit burns at a relatively low temperature and allows for a maximum amount of smoke to be absorbed into the meat without being cooked into oblivion. I use this smoker even in subfreezing temperatures with good results. In warm weather I do the smoking at night when the air is cooler.

River Salmon Fishing

When a new smoker is purchased, a bag of wood chips will be included. More of these chips can be purchased at most outdoor stores. These work great except for one problem. A panful is consumed within an hour. This means the pan must be fed fresh chips all too frequently.

We have a wood stove at our house and keep a large supply of firewood on hand. It is a simple matter to slice up alder, maple, cherry, or apple wood into pieces slightly smaller in diameter than the chip pan. One of these slices one and a half inches thick will smoke for seven or eight hours. Some hickory chips stuffed in around the edges of an alder round make a nice combination. Under no circumstances should any soft wood be used since it will impart a strong taste to the fish.

One last word about the smoker; after each use, turn it upside down and make sure that all loose ash is dumped out. Each smoking session should be begun with a smoke pan from which all ash has been removed. The end product loses a little something if it has a light dusting of ash. If the racks become grundgy, they can be run through the electric dishwasher or soaked in some hot soapy water and then rinsed.

To make the brine, a plastic bucket or non-metallic crock or bowl large enough to hold 10 or 12 pounds of fish pieces is required. A glass plate slightly smaller in diameter than the bucket or bowl, a measuring cup and spoon, and a large stirring spoon complete the necessary equipment. The success of this recipe is dependent upon the *exact* measurement of the ingredients.

Into the container place precisely the following components:

> **One U.S. gallon of water**
> **2 cups of non-iodized salt**
> **1/2 cup brown sugar**
> **3/8 cup lemon juice**
> **1 teaspoon liquid garlic**
> **1 teaspoon liquid onion**

Stir until the salt and sugar are dissolved. This brine will impart a marvelous texture and flavor to the salmon.

Cleaning

Thoroughly clean the fish, removing head, tail, and as much of the blood and slime as possible. Some people prefer to smoke with the bones intact while others like the fish filleted before brining and smoking. Filleting beforehand helps in obtaining a uniform penetration of smoke. Leave the skin on the meat. The fish should be cut into pieces that will fit on the smoker's racks. Salmon that has been frozen accepts smoking very well.

Place the salmon pieces in the brine and give a thorough stirring. Lay the plate on top of the fish to insure that all pieces are completely submerged in the liquid. Leave for an hour and administer another stirring. After the fish has been in the brine for a total of two or two and a half hours, remove and thoroughly rinse each piece in cold water. Place on the racks skin-side down and allow the fish-laden racks to air dry on some newspapers for about an hour. A slight glaze or pellicle will form on the surface of the fish. The thinner pieces of meat should be arranged on the uppermost racks. Place the racks into the smoking frame, put wood into the pan, plug in and away you go.

The length of time that the salmon is left in the smoker will depend on the air temperature and how moist one likes his smoked fish. I usually plug it in at bedtime and check it in the morning. Keep adding wood as long as the smoker is plugged in. Cold temperatures may require smoking for up to 24 hours. Disconnect when it is done to your preference.

There are countless brine recipes and some are excellent. Once the neophyte catches on to the idiosyncracies of his smoker, he undoubtedly will want to try some innovative touches. The above recipe works every time and the results are at least as good as the finest commercially-smoked salmon.

Grav–Laks

If you have Viking blood in your veins or enjoy the comic strip character, Hagar the Horrible, you might like Grav-Laks.

River Salmon Fishing

About the only restaurants in which I've experienced this delightful dish are at Horst Magar's Tivoli Gardens and L'Omlette restaurants in Portland, Oregon. I've observed that the hungry crowds at the famous Sunday brunches devour this delicacy very rapidly.

The tools needed are a long narrow dish with a tight lid and a super sharp slicing knife. There is a model of Tupperware container that fits this requirement but if one is not available, the narrow dish may be covered with handiwrap.

The salmon must be very fresh. Remove head, tail, and fillet away all bones and fins. Leave the skin. Cut the two fillets into lengths short enough to fit inside the dish.

For an average-size salmon, make a mixture of three cups of non-iodized salt and two cups of turbinado (raw sugar). If turbinado is not available at your health food store, use brown sugar. Coat the flesh side of each fillet heavily with this mixture. If available, sprinkle each fillet with fresh dill. If dill is out of season, use dry dill weed.

Lay the fillets meat side to meat side in the dish and cover tightly. Place the dish in the refrigerator. After about 12 hours turn the fillets over, keeping them facing meat side to meat side. A brine will be forming in the bottom of the dish. Depending on the thickness of the fillet, leave in the covered dish for another 12 to 24 hours. Thick slabs require a longer processing. Take the fillets from the dish and drain. Remove any excess salt and sugar by patting the fish with a paper towel. The fillets will have shrunk to about half their original thickness.

Lay the fillet on a cutting board and with the sharp knife held at a 45-degree angle, slice into very thin strips cutting towards the tail.

These thin strips go down very nicely when placed on top of cream cheese spread on a sesame cracker or bagel.

Filleting

At sport shows and fish processing plants I've watched some experts fillet several kinds of fish. Those who make make a living at it can really wield a knife and waste very little meat as the sharp edge quickly contours the bone structure.

The less skilled will leave a lot of succulent meat on the bones. Even those who have had a great deal of practice can be a little sloppy in the filleting process.

A couple of years ago at a sport show I watched a fishing guide who had been pressed into making a fish cleaning demonstration. His credentials for putting a large number of fish into the boat were impeccable. He also knew all the standard cuts to make when filleting a fish. After the demonstration I hefted the discarded skeleton. He had left well over a pound of the 12-pounder's flesh on the bones.

Most of us will only be filleting a salmon or two at a time and a few extra minutes spent on the job won't be missed. It is imperative that the fillet knife be of good quality and very sharp.

River Salmon Fishing

Begin by gutting the fish and removing the head just below the gills. Also cut off the tail. Holding the fish on its back with the head end facing you, insert the point of the knife near the backbone and next to the rib bones. Insert the knife a couple of inches and follow the curve of the rib cage towards the belly. The knife will run out of bone to follow well before it reaches the incision made to remove the entrails. Allow the knife to cut through the belly lining. Insert the point up the backbone a couple of inches more and again slice along the contour of the rib bones until the blade comes through the belly lining. Continue the process to a point just behind the vent. The fillet will fall away from the bared rib cage.

Turn the fish end for end. Insert the knife's point a couple of inches along the backbone and slice upward until the knife comes through the skin. Keep inserting the knife, slicing upward until the point is reached just behind the anus. The caudal fin will remain on the skeleton.

The lower extremities of the fish are now clear of the bones. With the fish still lying on its back, start at the tail of the fish, roll the point of the knife over the bulge of the backbone and keeping the edge in contact with the resistance of the bone, slice until the knife comes through the skin in the middle of the back. Keep slicing a couple of inches at a time until the head end is reached. If the knife hugs the bone, there will be an almost bare side of a skeleton. The ventral fins will still be attached to the fillet. Theoretically, the adipose and dorsal fins will be sliced in half lengthwise, but practically speaking they are usually left attached, intact, to one of the fillets. The process is repeated on the other side of the fish.

If the salmon is to be skinned, a sharp fillet knife with a blade a couple of inches longer than the breadth of the fillet is required. All fins should be removed before skinning. The fillet is laid on the cutting board skin side down. A slight cut is made parallel and next to the skin at the tail end of the fillet. Hopefully, by pressing down firmly with your thumb against the skin, the skin will be held in place while the meat is removed. If it slips, a fork will pin the skin to the board. With a sawing action,

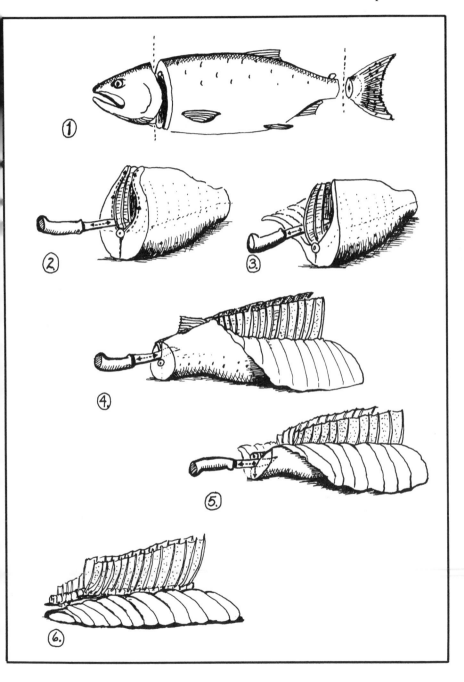

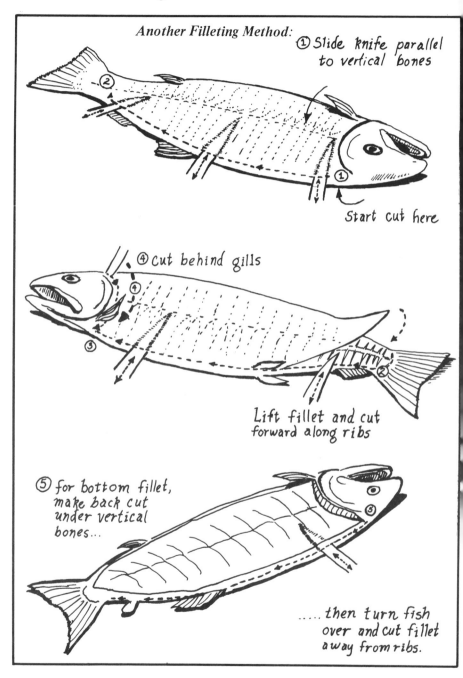

Another Filleting Method:

① Slide knife parallel to vertical bones

Start cut here

④ Cut behind gills

Lift fillet and cut forward along ribs

⑤ for bottom fillet, make back cut under vertical bones...

.....then turn fish over and cut fillet away from ribs.

work the blade along the skin to the head end of the fish. A beautiful piece of meat will come away from the skin in one piece.

If the fish is going to the taxidermist, it should not be cleaned. Immediately, after dispatching the fish, take several color photos to aid the taxidermist in recreating the fish's natural coloration. Measure the length and girth just in front of the dorsal. If possible, freeze the fish in the round. Should there be no freezer available, wrap the trophy in a burlap bag or sheet and keep as cool as possible.

Kerry Burkheimer and guide Val Perry with two fall chinook from Oregon's coastal Chetco River.

Salmon Poisoning Disease

Each year thousands of unfortunate dogs in western Washington, Oregon, and California are afflicted with Salmon Poisoning Disease. If left untreated most of these dogs would die. The disease is caused by a virus-like organism present in raw or cold-smoked salmon and steelhead. Humans are not affected by the virus.

Thorough cooking or freezing of the fish for two weeks kills the disease-causing organisms. Under no circumstances should entrails, heads, skeletons, or other raw salmon parts be left where they can be eaten by dogs.

The symptoms of a disease-infected dog are similar to those of distemper. Sometime, in a period of 6 to 20 days after eating infested fish, the animal will experience a rise in body temperature. Soon after, there will be a loss of appetite, listlessness, vomiting, and diarrhea.

If not treated by a veterinarian, most dogs will be dead within two weeks.

Where To Fish: California

Despite its huge population, California has been able to maintain some very good salmon fishing. An effective hatchery system and aggressive fisheries management have resulted in reconstituted runs of fish. Destruction of habitat seems to have stabilized and careful regulation should result in good fishing for future generations.

The 400-mile-long Sacramento River is the biggest salmon attraction in California. Some 30 resorts plus numerous nearby motels provide accommodations along the river. There are fall, winter, and spring runs of chinook. Some of these fish may reach 50 pounds. Because of the large size of the river, a boat is required to reach most of the water.

The Eel hosts substantial runs of fall chinook in September and October. A small run of coho also enters this river in October.

During the period from August through October numerous chinook ascend the Klamath River and provide some very good fishing. The main tributaries are the Trinity, Salmon, Scott, and the Shasta rivers and these all host parts of the Klamath's bounty. A small run of silvers also enters the Klamath in October.

The Smith is the northernmost salmon river in California and is famous for its chinook in September and October. Some individual fish exceed 50 pounds. This river has been very popular for fly fishermen as well as lure and bait casters.

Where To Fish: Oregon

O regon is fortunate to be blessed with numerous rivers capable of producing runs of salmon. The fishing year begins in late January when early arriving spring chinook are caught in the Willamette and ends with bright winter runs in December in the Elk and Sixes.

Additional major salmon rivers include the Alsea, Chetco, Clackamas, Deschutes, Columbia, Nestucca, Rogue, Sandy, Trask, Umpqua, and Wilson.

For a very detailed listing of the timing and numbers of salmon in Oregon's many rivers, I would suggest obtaining a copy of *Steelhead and Salmon Sport Catch Statistics* published by Frank Amato Publications. This book is a compilation of the punch card and creel census records by the Oregon Department of Fish and Wildlife.

Where To Fish: Washington

B ecause of the heavy Indian netting allowed by the Boldt Decision, many of Washington's salmon rivers are subject to severe restrictions for sports anglers. Unnetted rivers outside the area covered in Boldt's decision offer some excellent fishing. The Cowlitz, Kalama, and North Lewis host good runs of both spring and fall chinook. The lower Klickitat also has a good run of spring chinook.

Coho are available in the Washougal, North Lewis, Kalama, Cowlitz, Elochoman, Grays, Naselle, and Willapa rivers.

Where To Fish: British Columbia

B ritish Columbia has led the way in fine tuning sport fishing regulations. Bait, treble hooks, and barbed hooks are banned in many areas. Only chinook and coho may be taken in fresh water. A careful examination of the Fishing Regulation is required to determine the open season and regulations for each river. Some of the more popular rivers include the Lakelse, Bulkley, Dean, Big Qualicum, Skeena, and Anarko. Most small coastal streams have a run of coho.

Hatcheries

D ue to man's destruction of their habitat and overfishing of the resource, there would be few salmon today in our populated areas if it were not for an ever-increasing hatchery program. Unfortunately, it is highly unlikely that in the foreseeable future, at least, that sufficient rebuilding of the runs can be accomplished without the multitude of eggs that can be hatchery produced. Besides, it seems that some of our fish managers are fearful that a few salmon will escape the artificially-structured spawning runs and attempt to spawn naturally without the assistance of hatchery personnel. Mother Nature intended that salmon should die in the river and that their decaying bodies provide the nutrients necessary to complete the life cycle.

It is not necessary that every fish be harvested at a hatchery and sold for human and animal consumption. It seems plausible that more spawning channels creating semi-natural conditions could be constructed adjacent to the hatcheries' fish ladders to accommodate fish that are surplus to the egg gathering process. The Canadians have had considerable success with spawning channels where the fish are never touched by human hands. This approach has been largely ignored by American fish managers.

Jim Teeny puts back a beautiful chinook.

River Salmon Fishing

Of the coho currently being harvested in Oregon, only about 15% are wild fish. Sixty percent are being produced by federal and state hatcheries and 25% are being released by private salmon ranchers.

The first salmon hatchery was built at Orland, Maine in 1871. This was an attempt to preserve an already dwindling population of Atlantic salmon. The following year a Pacific salmon hatchery was constructed on California's McCloud River. Some of the eggs were shipped eastward to the Susquehanna River where they all perished.

In 1887, the Northwest received its first salmon hatchery when a facility was installed on the Clackamas River in Oregon.

By the turn of the century there were 15 salmon hatcheries in the State of Washington. Today there is a hatchery on almost every stream in the Northwest large enough to host a salmon run. Many of these hatcheries have been built by government agencies as mitigation and restitution measures for loss of salmon spawning grounds caused by dam construction.

Canada, because of its smaller population of humans and less rapid exploitation of the environment, was slower to develop an intensive hatchery system. Unfortunately, the steady encroachment of man overtook the Canadian salmon's ability to maintain its runs by natural spawning and today there are about 40 salmon hatcheries in British Columbia.

Because little was known of the various salmon's life cycles, the early attempts at artificial reproduction were relatively unsuccessful. As biologists learned more about the wild fish's residence in fresh water, they were able to create a compatible environment for the eggs, alevins, fry, fingerlings, and smolts that would prepare them for their migration to the sea.

The major breakthrough came when trial and error proved that larger fish had a much better chance of survival. Larger migrants are better able to forage for food and defend themselves against predators.

Increased knowledge of the cycle allowed artificial growth stimulation and genetic selection. The goal of course is to produce the maximum number and quality of fish for the dollar.

The author in the 1950s with an Alaska fly-caught coho salmon.

River Salmon Fishing

The first step in the hatchery cycle is procuring mature fish. Most modern hatcheries have some type of fish trap and holding pond where the returning fish may be kept to maturity. If no fish trap is available or if fish management wishes to tap a wild native run, a seine is used to capture free swimming fish. In a few instances fish difficult to procure by net are caught by hook and line and placed in a holding pond until maturity.

Hatchery programs have helped to mitigate for many wild salmon runs that were destroyed by dams, logging and other causes.

When it is determined that the fish are ripe, the females are anesthetized. Their bellies are slit and the eggs poured into a sterilized bucket. The male's milt is milked over the eggs and stirred. Size selection of both males and females may have some important bearing on the size and age of the progeny.

The fertilized eggs are placed in sterilized trays and washed with cold water. As the incubation progresses, the eggs are constantly sorted to insure that only the viable ones are present. The length of the incubation period will be dependent upon the temperature of the water that flows over them. Very cold water retards growth. The alevins remain in their trays for 6 to 8 weeks while their egg sacs are being absorbed. Coho and chinook fry are fed finely ground meat. As they become larger, moist pellets become their source of food. Modern hatcheries utilize automatic feeders controlled by electronic timers. Modern feeding and handling techniques have resulted in producing one pound of young fish for each 1.7 pounds of feed. When the hatcheries were in their infancy many, many pounds of feed were used to produce a pound of fish.

Because of the high mortality rate of the young fish, it costs the taxpayers about $15.00 to produce a mature coho. If a commercial troller catches this fish, he can sell it for about $9.00. If the coho is landed by a sports fisherman, approximately $100.00 will have been spent to finance the capture.

Smoltification determines the timing of the release of the young coho and to some extent that of the chinook. Too early or too late into the metamorphosis of the young fish results in a reduced return. A successful hatchery program depends on producing smolts that immediately begin their descent to the sea. Rapidly departing smolts also compete less for the available food with the wild juveniles already present in the stream.

Transformation into smolthood utilizes most of the stored body fat of the little fish. Delay in reaching the abundant feeding opportunities of the salt or estuary can be fatal. Nature has taken another step in aiding the descent to the sea. When the little fish is a stream dweller, it spends most of its time holding close to the bottom. During the smolting process the swim bladder partially fills with air. This critical part of the metamorphosis greatly increases the fish's buoyancy and allows its seaward drift with minimum effort.

Young chinooks will usually be released into the river after a few months of life in the hatchery. Their smoltification seems to occur gradually as they descend their river. Coho are held until smolthood occurs at about one year. However, accelerated feeding conditions have resulted in coho smolts large enough to migrate after only a few months of hatchery life. Chum fry are released immediately after the egg sac is absorbed.

River Salmon Fishing

The descending hatchery young have not been subjected to that important natural phenomenon experienced by their wild counterparts. . . the survival of the fittest. Their chances of completing their life cycle will be greatly influenced by the hatchery's water supply, food, timing, and presence of disease. If all conditions and timing are right, a reasonable percentage will survive the many hazards encountered and return to produce fertilized eggs for future generations.

Marty Sherman, Editor of FLYFISHING magazine, holds a live Alaska coho salmon.

Possibly the best performance on spring chinook has been attained by planting rather large 7- to 8-inch smolts in the Umpqua River. The return from the initial plant exceeded 9%.

Returns of this magnitude are rare, however. Most hatchery managers would be delighted if 5% of the plant made it back to their facility.

Modern man can do much to enhance and restore the salmon runs that his predecessors unthinkingly destroyed. Hatcheries aren't the only answer. Streams can be re-opened by removal of log jams and rock barriers. Fish ladders can provide a migratory path around existing waterfalls. Former spawning and nursery areas can be cleared of collected debris and trash. Spawning gravel removed by floods and road building can be replaced. Cattle grazing along the river banks can be curtailed and the damaged river edges reseeded. Fish ladders can be built or improved to enable ascending fish to circumnavigate existing dams. Reduced netting will allow more fish to reach the spawning gravel.

The Oregon Department of Fish and Wildlife has implemented an innovative program called "Salmon and Trout Enhancement Program (STEP). The object of STEP is to involve private citizens, groups, clubs, and businesses in enhancement activities. The program was conceived to produce a maximum of effort for a minimum of cash by utilizing volunteer labor and donated materials. The program is guided by an advisory committee and all projects are designed and supervised by Fish and Wildlife personnel. The activities include many of the ways of enhancement mentioned in the paragraph above. In addition, widespread use of streamside egg incubator boxes and the Whitlock-Vibert box have utilized eggs that were surplus to the hatchery system's needs.

Aquaculture

The aquaculture concept actually began in the United States in the late nineteenth century when private concerns built salmon hatcheries on the Rogue and Clackamas rivers in Oregon. By 1900, the government had assumed the responsibility of artificially propagating salmon.

River Salmon Fishing

Japan and Russia have been steadily increasing their aquaculture activities for the last couple of decades. Oregon, California, Alaska, Washington, and British Columbia are more recent participants in this rapidly expanding industry.

Egg production is the current limiting factor in the growth of salmon farming. Until recently, the egg availability in the United States was limited to what was determined to be surplus by the government hatcheries. Aquaculture companies are now producing some of their own eggs and purchase of eggs from Russia has been approved by the federal government.

Before man started to harvest the world's salmon, limitations on the numbers of fish was determined by the amount and quality of spawning areas. As the spawning sites were gradually, but relentlessly, destroyed by man, the salmon population plumetted. Salmon ranching allows the production of fish without the use of spawning gravel.

If disease-free juveniles can be sent out to sea to feed, complete their normal growing cycle, and return as valuable adults, it would seem that the numbers of returning fish would be limited only by the amount of feed available in the ocean. The casual observer might also be under the impression that there will only be positive results from introducing these hordes of artificially reared salmon into the oceans' feeding areas.

Many sportsmen and biologists are concerned that the increased numbers of maturing salmon in the seas will accelerate the commercial fishing effort and will further reduce the already-threatened runs of wild salmon and steelhead.

Because the return sites of the farmed fish are largely saltwater locations, few of these salmon are available to the river fisherman. Of course, there will be some straying which will result in an undetermined number of fish venturing up our rivers in an attempt to reproduce naturally. Sport fishermen able to ply the salt waters adjacent to the aquaculture return sites have been successful in catching large numbers of the farm-produced adult fish.

In spite of the fact that American trollers have harvested large numbers of aquaculturally produced salmon, they are largely opposed to the concept. Their fears seem to stem from a belief that a successful aquaculture industry on the eastern rim of the Pacific will produce large numbers of low-priced salmon that will force them out of business. This is a distinct possibility. So far, American salmon farming has not been profitable. The situation is far different in Japan and Russia, however. State-run fish farms in Russia and private and government facilities in Japan have reaped the bounty of the sea in the form of the return of millions of adults in recent years. Both countries plan to crescendo their programs in the next decade to the point where their adult harvest will be well into the billions.

Japan has been very effective in its efforts to ranch salmon. Their most successful hatchery has been able to produce a mature chum salmon for about a dollar and a half. This is about one-sixth of its market value. Should saturation of the world's market eventually occur and efficiency increase, greatly reduced prices could result.

The type of facility required for salmon farming varies among the species and races within the species. The pinks and chums, which in the wild normally begin their seaward migration soon after hatching, are the least expensive to produce. The fish farm simply has to hold the newly hatched fry at the return site for a couple of weeks to insure that the area's release site is imprinted on the fish and then send those babies out to sea.

Some races of chinook and sockeye also migrate soon after hatching and could be adapted to low cost fish farming.

Coho, some chinook, most sockeye, Japan's masu, and the Atlantic salmon all have to experience smolthood before being released into the sea. Feeding these fish for several months and providing suitable environment for them during this period adds greatly to their cost.

Fish culturists have been able to accelerate the smolting process of salmon by carefully regulating the water temperature of the rearing pens. Attempts continue to lower the feed cost by utilizing the waste by-products of poultry and fish processing plants. These efforts have resulted in producing coho smolts in six months rather than the normal 12- to 18-month period.

Some are wondering just how much food is swimming around in the Pacific for all of these farmed salmon to eat. The salmon farming situation is complicated by intense commercial fishing for squid and herring — two principal ingredients in the diet of salmon. Other fish such as hake also savagely compete for the existing food. Of course, big salmon eat little salmon, too. Only time will tell how the food supply will adapt to this relatively new industry.

Where To Fish: Alaska

A s a general rule, and there is some variation, the chinooks are the first salmon to enter Alaska's rivers and the cohos are the last. The chum and sockeye will be right behind the chinooks. The pinks will generally be slightly ahead of the cohos. Some rivers have early and late runs of a species.

Particularly hospitable rivers have all five varieties and will almost continuously have fresh runs of some species from June until well into September. A few rivers will host all five species simultaneously.

In the rivers flowing into Bristol Bay, the kings will start migrating in early June and continue through July. The chums and sockeye will enter early in July and keep coming into the first part of August. In even-numbered years pinks begin their run in July and populate the rivers well into August. The cohos begin their runs in late July and will still be coming in September. There are lots of exceptions.

Chinooks and chums that have a long way to migrate will start their upstream journey as soon as the ice breaks up.

The distance that the spawning area is from salt water will also greatly affect the natatorial speed. Some salmon runs seem to dawdle along the way while others make great haste to reach their natal domicile. Local knowledge is essential to insure that the angler will be on the water when the desired species is present.

In south central Alaska the chinook will migrate somewhat earlier than in the Bristol Bay region. The Kenai River has a run of spring chinook that enter soon after ice-out in May. Additional runs arrive in June and July.

The fishing possibilities and depth of the wilderness experience are extremely varied in Alaska. The quantities of available salmonids are beyond the comprehension of the angler who has not enjoyed fishing in this relatively remote state. Individual rivers will host more salmon than the entire remnant Atlantic salmon populations of Europe and North America.

For those who like the luxury of a modern motel and restaurant meals and lots of people, salmon fishing is available along the main highway on the Kenai Peninsula. Many guides are available on the Kenai River in the Soldotna area and non-fishing members of the family can watch television or go shopping.

A slightly more rustic approach would be to use one of the

River Salmon Fishing

many campgrounds along the rather limited road system. RVs and camping equipment may be rented in Anchorage.

The main problem with the above two approaches is people. Upon arriving by automobile at a river experiencing a hot salmon bite, one will discover that a lot of other tourists have the same idea. In addition, half the population of Anchorage has been waiting all year for the opportunity to fill their freezers with salmon. If these conditions are agreeable with your life style and expectations, then by all means live the experience. The Kenai River probably produces the largest race of chinook salmon in the world. In addition, hordes of coho and reds swim up its slightly milky, glacial flow.

The confluence of the Russian and Kenai rivers provides one of the most intense fisheries in Alaska. The two runs of readily-caught sockeye that home into the Russian attract fishermen from around the world. Many motels and resorts provide accommodations for the automobile-transported tourists.

Further along the Kenai Peninsula are the Anchor and Ninilchik. Both of these fine streams have good runs of kings and silvers.

To the north of Anchorage, the auto-travelling fisherman can fish for kings in Caswell, Montana, and Willow Creeks. No road traverses the west side of the glacial Sustina River and access to the fine fishing for kings and silvers in the Deshka River, Alexander and Lake creeks is accessible by jet boat or float plane only.

A relatively low cost, semi-wilderness trip can be had by driving to Talkeetna and hiring a jet boat for transportation up the rough-and-tumble, silty Talkeetna River to the mouth of Clear Creek. This watershed supports runs of kings, silvers, sockeyes, and pinks.

In the Copper River area the Gulkana, Klutina, and Copper rivers offer fishing for kings.

There are several very fine fishing lodges scattered throughout Alaska. The available accommodations vary from luxurious to adequate. The site that is selected would depend upon the individual's desires and finances. If a daily hot shower is necessary to your well-being and peace of mind, an inquiry to your prospective host will determine if this type of convenience is available.

Many of the remote rivers are owned by the natives and permanent lodges are not permitted on some. Permits to erect tent camps have been obtained by some outfitters. These can be very comfortable and their portability can make some great fishing accessible. Some of the more elaborate camps of this type have excellent equipment that includes hot showers and everything necessary to make the guest's stay very comfortable.

A nice, full-bodied coho salmon that was tricked by a fly. Marty Sherman photo

River Salmon Fishing

Another possibility would be to rent a small cabin through the U.S. Forest Service. There are several such facilities available and can result in a true wilderness experience. Some of these remote cabins have a gasoline stove and lantern and users fly in and out in a float plane.

Bristol Bay and Kuskokwim Bay have so many rivers flowing into them that more than a lifetime would be required to explore them all. Jet fields at King Salmon, Dillingham and Bethel serve this fish-laden paradise. All five species are present in many of the rivers. Kings, silvers, chums, pinks, and sockeye are numerous in the Alagnak, Nushagak, Goodnews, Kanektok, Mulchatna, Togiak, Naknek, and Wood systems. The Kvichak boasts runs of sockeye totaling millions as well as numerous chums and silvers.

For those wishing to go further north, the Unalakleet River, which flows into Norton Sound, has runs of all five species.

In southeastern Alaska, chinooks may not be fished in most freshwater. However, outstanding river fishing for silvers is available in several streams near Yakutat and Ketchikan.

The more adventurous may want to take a float trip down one of Alaska's beautiful pristine rivers. There are several competent outfitters that conduct this type of trip and have adequate equipment to insure a really fine experience.

It is also possible for a group to make a float trip entirely on their own. This alternative should be undertaken only by experienced outdoorsmen and boatmen, and inquiry should be made beforehand about regulations and access availability.

Alaska has a large population of bears, and a few of these resent intrusion of their private fishing grounds by other bears or humans. If you decide to make the trip on your own, be sure to pack a heavy rifle or slug-stuffed 12-gauge shotgun. It is very unlikely that an angry bear is going to be stopped with a 44 Magnum revolver.

Carrying a gun is a serious responsibility and under no circumstances should it be used to harass or frighten the bears. A decision should be made beforehand at the minimum distance that the bear will be allowed to approach. If the bear knows of your presence, is on all fours, and is coming rapidly in your direction, one had better start firing at 25 or 30 feet.

What Not To Do!

We were just finishing a late dinner at the Alagnak Lodge after a great day's fishing when four very sorry looking characters came limping up to the front door. There was the weary look of defeat in their expressions.

It had rained most of the day and they were completely soaked and bedraggled. The disheveled group looked around at the clean, dry, and warm lounge and asked if they could spend the night.

These fellows resided in a southern state and had decided to take an Alaskan adventure on their own. They evidently had done little research concerning the necessary items for a successful and pleasant trip. The Bristol Bay area is rugged, isolated country and like most of Alaska, should only be attempted with the best possible equipment.

Most of the gear that they had brought probably would have served them fine for a summer's weekend outing in Texas, but was very inadequate for the rigors of Alaska. Their two tents leaked. The down sleeping bags and parkas were soggy lumps and their plastic rain jackets had been shredded on the first walk through the brush. One of the party had packed an Avon inflatable boat and it was about the only piece of equipment that was adequate. Their other craft was a cheap plastic affair that had suffered many perforations and was generously spotted with multicolored patches. The two unfortunates who were paddling this frail mistake had been wet from the waist down for a week. Much of the time that should have been available for fishing and enjoying the scenery was spent in patching the boat.

These fellows had flown into King Salmon by jet and hired a bush pilot to fly them into Kukaklek Lake and pick them up at the mouth of the Alagnak River. No effort had been made to fly the length of the river to check for log jams and rapids.

Unarmed, they had spent a couple of sleepless nights when they had been terrorized by brown bears that resented their trespass. Their diluted insect repellent had little effect on the ravenous mosquitos and white stockings.

The fishing tackle that they possessed had been designed for bass and crappies and the few salmon that were hooked had demolished their inadequate rods and reels.

The lodge manager turned on the hot showers, gave them medicine for their mosquito bites and white stocking wounds. A little wine and a hot supper gave them a warm glow. They wearily crawled into warm, dry bunks.

The next morning they were completely different human beings with revitalized attitudes. They asked if they could go fishing until their pick-up plane arrived. Ernie, the lead guide, gave them a cram course on how to catch a salmon and had them on the river in a few minutes.

Outfitted with the proper equipment and fortified with a little education, they caught several salmon in the next few hours. Their disaster was converted into a fish story with a happy ending. They wrote a check for a week's fishing for the next year before departing.

Bears love salmon too, and generally take precedent over other anglers along British Columbia and Alaska streams. Jim Teeny photo

141

Alaska: Equipment — (Casting/Spinning)

be required to stop powerful runs. If the fishing will be from a boat and the salmon can be chased, a little lighter tackle can be used.

Casting/Spinning (Chinook Salmon)

Rod: Lamiglas G1318T or G1316T Casting or other quality rod

Reel: Shimano TRN 200 G or Quantum Pro 4

  or: Lamiglas G1319 Spinning

       Penn 650 or 850SS or other quality reel

Dai Riki Monofilament 30 or 36 lb. test or,

Maxima Monofilament 20 or 25 lb. test

Extra line

Leader Wheels 46 lb. Dai Riki or 30 lb. Maxima

Rosco Snap Swivels Size 7 or 5

Pencil lead 1/4"

Pixee 7/8 oz. Hammered Brass/Orange, Hammered Nickel/Red

Spin-N-Glo Kits Size 2 or Size 0 Pink, Flame, Pearl/Red

Hot Shot 025 Orange, Silver, Blue Pirate

Magnum Wiggle Wart

Tee Spoon #5 and Skagit Special #6

Vibrax Spinner Size 6 Silver, Silver/Red

Mepps Giant Killer

Single Siwash Hooks 3/0 and 4/0

Hook File and Lure Box

Scissors or Clippers

Polarized Fishing Glasses

Long Nose Pliers and Swiss Army Knife

Fishing Vest or Hip Pack

Casting/Spinning (Chums, Silvers, Sockeyes)

Rods: Lamiglas G1306T Casting or other quality rod
Reels: Quantum 1420
  or: Lamiglas G1307 Spin
       Penn 4500SS or other quality reel
Dai Riki Monofilament 19 lb. test or
       Maxima Monofilament 12 lb. test
Extra Line
Dai Riki Leader Wheels 15 and 19 test
Rosco Snap Swivels Size 10 and 7
Pixee 1/2 oz. and 7/8 oz. Silver/Red, Silver/Green
Steelee 1/2 oz. Metallic Green, HB/FL Stripe, HN/FL
Little Cleo 3/4 oz.
Maribou Jigs 1/4 oz. Red/White, Pink
Mepps Silver and Gold Size 5
Rooster Tail 1/2 oz. Flame
Tee Spoon Size 4
Vibrax Size 5 Silver, Silver/Green, Silver/Red
Twist On Lead Strips and Split Shot
Hook File
Lure Box
Scissors or Clippers
Polarized Fishing Glasses
Long Nose Pliers
Swiss Army Knife
Fishing Vest or Hip Pack
Single Siwash Hooks 1/0, 2/0, 3/0

Alaska: Equipment — Fly Fishing

Fly fishing for chinooks should be done with an AFTMA 9 or 10-weight outfit. A fighting butt is highly recommended. A Teeny T300 or T400 sink-tip line will probably be required to get the fly down to the fish. At least 200 yards of 30-pound backing will be required to stop these heavy fish. Leaders with 20-pound-test tippets are adequate. It may be necessary to wrap a little lead wire on the leader to help sink the fly to the fish's depth. Careful selection of a high quality, large capacity reel is essential.

The pursuit of the other species can be handled with an 8-weight outfit. If just the small pinks are being fished, a No. 6 combination would be fine. A high quality fly reel capable of holding at least 150 yards of 20-pound-test backing will be necessary to stop the rambunctious silvers, sockeyes, and chums.

Both a floating and a very fast sinking line are useful. Because of the salmon's very sharp teeth, 12-pound tippets will prevent the rapid depletion of the fly inventory.

Because the Alaskan elements can be very rugged, it is essential to take top quality equipment. In most remote areas, replacement camping gear will not be available should yours fail. If one is staying at a lodge, of course, this is not a factor.

The commercial airlines are very generous with the amount of baggage that can be taken on board. They request that baggage be packed into containers weighing a maximum of 70 pounds each. To reduce the possibility of lost luggage, it is suggested that everything be checked to Anchorage, picked up, and hand-carried to the next flight departure point.

Most transportation beyond the airline terminals will be via single engine wheel or float plane. The amount of gear that can be transported in addition to the number of passengers should be checked with the pilot or flight service before leaving home.

The three basic dangers encountered by the camper are hypothermia, bears and insects. Of the three, hypothermia is the most serious. Assume that you are going to get wet and cold and insure that the necessary items are available to become dry and warm. Count on encountering lots of rain and chilling storms blown in from the North Pacific and Bering Sea. You will be delighted if these maladies decide to bypass your trip.

Adequate shelter, clothing, and heat can make all the difference.

The insect problem is easily controlled with a Shoo Bug Jacket or Muskol repellent. Forget or lose these items and a miserable experience is likely to occur.

Bears are numerous over much of Alaska. Just because a previous visitor to an area didn't see bears doesn't mean that one won't be present when your party arrives. If camping outside of a park, a heavy rifle or 12-gauge shotgun loaded with slugs should be available.

King Salmon

Rod: Lamiglas G1298-9, G1299-9 or G1298-10 or other
            quality rod

Reels: S.A. System II 1011 or 89 or other quality, strong reel

Extra Spool

Fly Line Backing 30 lb.

Teeny 300 and Wet Tip Lines

Tapered Leaders 15 and 20 lb. tippets

Dai Riki Leader Wheels .017 and .019

Twist On Lead and Split Shot

Hook File

Fly Box

Scissors or Clippers

Polarized Sun Glasses

Long Nose Pliers

Swiss Army Knife

Fishing Vest

Outrageous 4/0

Crazy Charlie Purple Pearl 4/0

Polar Shrimp 1/0

Teeny Nymph Size 2 Pink, Flame, Black or Ginger

Alaskabous, Pixees Revenge, Showgirl Size 1/0

Wiggle Tail, Orange or White Size 1/0

Chums, Silvers, Sockeyes

Rods: Lamiglas G1298-8 or other quality rod

Reels: S.A. System II 78, Hardy St. Aidan and Marguis 10 or
        other quality reel

Extra Spools

Fly Line Backing
Floating, Wet Tip and T300 Teeny Lines
Tapered Leaders 12 lb. Tippet
Dai Riki Leader Wheels .013 to .015
Twist On Lead Strips and Split Shot
Hook File
Fly Box
Scissors or Clippers
Polarized Fishing Glasses
Long Nose Pliers
Swiss Army Knife
Fishing Vest
Alaskan Bug Eyes Size 2
G String Size 2
Teeny Nymph Size 2 Pink, Flame, Black, Ginger
Babine Special Size 2 and 4
Skykomish Sunrise Size 2
Flash Fly 1/0
Polar Shrimp Size 2 and 4
Outrageous 1/0
Alaskabous, Show Girl, Pixee Revenge, Coho Size 1/0
Wiggle Tail Orange and White Size 1/0
Woolly Bugger Purple Size 2
Egg Sucking Leech Size 2 Purple or Black

Alaska Check List: Camping — Group
Tent: Good quality with insect proof netting, poles, and
         stakes; all seams should be sealed to insure that it is
         100 percent waterproof
Plastic ground tarp: for under tent
Waterproof tarp: for outside of tent
One hundred feet of nylon parachute cord
Ten feet of pliable wire
Duct tape
Plastic electricians tape
Nylon strapping tape

Candles or lantern and mantles
Two camping stoves, funnel, and fuel: two single burner stoves
    are better than one two-burner unit
Map of area enclosed in ziploc bag
Ax with leather sheath
G.I. folding shovel
Matches in waterproof container; and/or cigarette lighter
First aid kit
Cooking and eating utensils
Metal bucket for water and washing dishes
Soap and Brillo pads
Heavy rifle and ammo (30.06 minimum) or 12-gauge and slugs
Heavy-duty coolers strong enough to sit on
Plastic garbage bags: all burnable garbage should be burned;
    the rest packed out
Five-minute epoxy glue
Twelve large nails
Food and seasonings
Toilet tissue
Towels
Wader patching kit
Whisk broom
Paper towels
Can opener
Side cutter pliers
Screw driver
Fire starter
Shell insect strip

Check List: Camping — Individual
Holofil II or Qualofil sleeping bag and stuff bag
Foam mattress pad
Towel
Soap
Wash cloth
Fillet knife and sharpening stone; if fish are to be kept

Waterproof duffel bag
Nylon duffel bag
Leather gloves
Three wire coat hangers
Heavy-duty plastic garbage bag
Stocking cap

If not staying at a lodge where extra fishing tackle might be available, it is a good idea to take along an extra rod and reel.

Dress for winter steelhead fishing; clothing should be wool or polypropylene for quick drying. Down is a poor choice. A complete change of clothing is essential.

Waders: high quality neoprene with suspenders; or hip boots
Rainwear coat with hood; PVC nylon or waxed cotton
Camp shoes
Fishing license and copy of local fishing regulations
Single hooks in some areas
Sunglasses
Camera and film
Personal toilet articles
Hand lotion and Chapstick
Insect repellent; Shoo Bug Jacket and Muskol
Wool or neoprene fishing gloves
Medical prescriptions (if applicable)
Rod, reel, line and lures
Extra line
Hook file
Rod container (very durable)
Two wool shirts, two pairs of wool pants, wool socks, under
        wear, cap, wool sweater, jacket (polypropylene is
        excellent), long underwear of wool or polypropylene
Small flashlight
Glass defogger, if eyeglasses are worn
Pocket knife
Needle nose pliers